MW00761722

# THE STATES OF CAMPAIGN FINANCE REFORM

# THE STATES OF CAMPAIGN FINANCE REFORM

DONALD A. GROSS
and
ROBERT K. GOIDEL

THE OHIO STATE UNIVERSITY PRESS

Columbus

Copyright © 2003 by The Ohio State University
All rights reserved.

Library of Congress Cataloging-in-Publication Data

Gross, Donald A. (Donald August), 1950–
    The states of campaign finance reform / Donald A. Gross and Robert K. Goidel.
        p. cm
Includes bibliographical references and index.
    ISBN 0-8142-0924-6 (hc : acid-free) — ISBN 0-8142-5103-X (pb : acid-free) —
ISBN 0-8142-9003-5 (CD ROM)
    1. Campaign funds—United States.  2. Governors—United States—Elections.
3. Political campaigns—United States.   I. Goidel, Robert K., 1967–   II. Title.
JK1991 .G76 2003
324.7'8'0973—dc21

                                                                    2002154503

Cover design by Bookcomp, Inc.
Text design by Bookcomp, Inc.
Type set in Adobe Garamond
Printed by Thomson-Shore, Inc.

The paper used in this publication meets the minimum requirements of the American
National Standard for Information Science—Permanence of Paper for Printed Library
Materials. ANSI Z39.48–1992.

9 8 7 6 5 4 3 2 1

# Contents

# Tables and Figures

# Introduction

In Washington, D.C., the campaign finance charade has played out with each new session of Congress. Reform-minded legislators—the John McCains and Russ Feingolds of the world—map out relatively modest proposals aimed at curbing some of the worst abuses of the current system of raising and spending campaign dollars. And though there is often a great partisan divide in terms of identifying the vilest offenses and the most palatable reforms, there is also a considerable gnashing of teeth over a system that just doesn't seem to work the way it should. Amidst this cacophony of discontent, reform-minded legislators have struggled to find majorities large enough to overcome a Republican filibuster in the Senate or a presidential veto. Without the bankruptcy of the once mighty energy corporation Enron, and the subsequent publicity given to Enron's considerable political influence—much of which was bought and paid for with campaign contributions—these reform-minded legislators would have continued to struggle with, and would have most likely been frustrated, once again, by, the intransigence of Washington politics.

In the Senate, Mitch McConnell (R-KY) has earned a reputation as campaign finance reform's worst nightmare. Despite its apparent popularity,[1] McConnell willingly, even eagerly, leads the charge to defeat reform. Having finally failed in his efforts to keep campaign finance reform from becoming law, McConnell has already promised to be the lead plaintiff on the first constitutional challenge to the new law. On this point, McConnell contends that no one has ever been defeated for voting against, or working against, campaign finance reform. At least McConnell is honest in his opposition. Many of the legislators who vote in favor of reform are secretly pleased when reform efforts are defeated, appreciating McConnell's efforts even as they are officially recorded as his opposition. For nearly thirty years, campaign reform was discussed in the nation's capital, while only rarely materializing, with a priori knowledge that its enactment was improbable.[2] The consideration of reform temporarily appeased an increasingly cynical and alienated public while feeding the media establishment with sound bites on the evils of money. But, in the long run, it undoubtedly increased public cynicism and added to public alienation, even as it protected individual members of Congress who could claim to be in favor of reform without ever having to abide by its provisions.

In the spring of 2002, in the wake of the Enron scandal, the landscape of campaign finance reform was drastically altered as the most successful fundraiser in the history of American politics, President George W. Bush, signed into law the most significant federal campaign finance reform legislation since the post–Watergate reforms of the mid-1970s: McCain–Feingold aimed at curbing what many see as the most egregious problems in the current system of campaign finance, soft money and so-called issue advocacy campaigns. McCain–Feingold passed by a filibuster-proof sixty votes in the Senate—even though a mere six months earlier the legislation had appeared, once again, to be dead.[3] Just as the Teapot Dome and Watergate scandals moved reluctant politicos to pass reform legislation in the past, the fall of the corporate energy giant Enron changed the dynamics of reform efforts in Congress. Enron had made major contributions to President Bush and to numerous members of Congress, Republicans and Democrats alike. Where McCain–Feingold had appeared dead in the Republican-controlled House of Representatives, it now passed with 240 votes. And, where President Bush had opposed McCain–Feingold during his presidential campaign, he reluctantly signed it into law.

McCain–Feingold was a significant step toward addressing reformist concerns with soft money.[4] But the focus in Washington on McCain–Feingold left other issues of campaign finance reform in the shadows. In states as diverse as Arizona and Massachusetts, the drive for reform moved beyond discussion to real, tangible changes in state campaign finance laws, even before the Enron scandal became headline news. Where incumbent legislators resisted, reformers made use of the levers of direct democracy and took the case for reform directly to the people. "In 1996 alone, voters in Arkansas, California, Colorado, Maine, Massachusetts, Montana, and Nevada voted in favor of ballot initiatives affecting campaign finance."[5] Mitch McConnell may be correct in his assertion that opposition to reform has few, if any, electoral repercussions; but when citizens are given the opportunity to vote directly on campaign reform, reform generally wins. And in some cases, as in Massachusetts in 1998, it wins big.[6]

But winning is hardly the point; better, more competitive, more participatory elections are the point. Otherwise reform is at best symbolism without substance, and at worst, a hindrance to democratic governance. Yet gauging the electoral consequences of reform is an exercise fraught with the potential for error. In this respect, elections are complex social and political phenomena — of which campaign financing plays only a part. In some elections, the race for campaign dollars plays a major role; in others, it plays a secondary or even tertiary role, trumped by issues of character, scandal, and incumbency. To understand the effects of campaign finance reform on the political process, one must begin by acknowledging that reform has both considerable promise and considerable limitations.

## GOVERNOR JESSE VENTURA: THE PROMISE OF REFORM

In contemporary politics, no figure has done more to galvanize public opinion than Jesse "The Body" Ventura. His surprise victory in Minnesota in 1998 sent shockwaves through the political establishment. Political commentators and experts alike have struggled with the meaning of his election: Was he a harbinger of things to come? Was there some great political unrest lurking just below the surface of economic tranquility? Or was he a statistical aberration, a one-time chance occurrence? Politics has long attracted its own assortment of former actors, astronauts, and television weathermen, but there was something different about this former professional wrestler, talk show host, mayor, and Navy Seal; something more populist, more crass, more profane. But whatever one thinks about the meaning of his election, this much is clear: Without public financing, there would have been no Governor Ventura.

Despite an uncanny ability to attract free media coverage, the Ventura campaign was never very successful at raising money, a fact that belies arguments that campaign contributions seek out attractive, electable candidates. By mid-summer, it was questionable whether the Ventura campaign would be able to raise enough money to qualify for public financing. Having raised only $12,000 by mid-July, the campaign needed to raise an additional $35,000 by the end of August in contributions of $50 or less to qualify for public funding.[7] In addition, because Ventura was running as a third party candidate, there were no guarantees that public funding would be forthcoming. The public financing provisions in Minnesota's law provides monies be granted to third party candidates retroactively, and then only if they receive at least 5 percent of the vote. So the total amount of money allocated to the Ventura campaign would be based on the campaign's showing in the general election. This uncertainty meant that the Ventura campaign would have to secure loans which could then be paid back after the election.[8] With public opinion polls indicating that Ventura's grassroots campaign was taking hold, the campaign was able to secure $330,000 in loans which in turn allowed Ventura to take his campaign to the television airwaves. The ads, which, among other things, portrayed Jesse Ventura as an action figure hero, netted him additional free local and national news coverage and was critical to his election as governor. As political scientist Steven Schier wrote about the Ventura candidacy, "Campaign finance laws do have consequences. No public money, no ads, no victory."[9]

In Minnesota, public financing helped transform Jesse Ventura from a media sideshow into the state's highest elected official. But the promise of reform, illustrated by Jesse Ventura's election, is much larger than a personal victory for a third party candidate. Campaign finance reform as an ideal offers the possibility that candidates outside of the mainstream, who may be judged unelectable by traditional funding sources, can get at least enough funding to be electorally viable. Campaign finance reform, in the ideal, offers the possibility that the Jesse Venturas of the political world will at least get a hearing, and that once heard, a few may even win.

## REFORM IN KENTUCKY: A TALE OF TWO ELECTIONS

If Jesse Ventura represents the possibility of reform, the experience in Kentucky over the past two gubernatorial elections represents both its promise and its limitations. Like many Southern states, Kentucky has long been a bastion of Democratic Party strength, with Republicans only recently gaining ground. Registered Democrats continue to outnumber Republicans by a rate of about 2 to 1. Until the Republican Party finally gained control of the Kentucky Senate in 1999 as a result of two state senators switching parties, the Democrats had held a majority in both houses of the Kentucky legislature for the entire twentieth century. Further, Kentucky had not elected a Republican governor since 1967. The partisan imbalance in the state, and the fact that governors were prohibited from seeking reelection, was very much reflected in how gubernatorial elections were conducted in the state prior to 1992. The Democratic Party primary was seen as the major step to becoming governor. Democratic primaries were crowded, competitive, and expensive. Republican primaries that were expensive and had more than one major candidate were an exception. In general elections, Republican gubernatorial candidates were historically underfunded and, subsequently, fared poorly.

In 1992, the Public Financing Campaign Act was passed by the Kentucky General Assembly and signed into law by the governor. The act serves as a good example of the type of comprehensive campaign finance reform that has been enacted in a number of states in recent years. First, the law placed strict new limits on the size of contributions to gubernatorial campaigns. Individuals, PACs (political action committees), and state or county executive committees of a political party were limited to contributions of no more than $500 for any one election.[10] Prior to 1992, such contributions were limited to $4,000 for any one election. The law also continued Kentucky's ban on contributions from corporations and labor unions. Limits on the use of personal loans by candidates were put in force. And finally, candidates were prohibited from receiving any contribution later than twenty-eight days before the election of interest.[11]

A second important component of the Kentucky law was the creation of the Registry of Election Finance. The Registry is an independent agency composed of seven members. Four members are appointed by the governor, while the Auditor of Public Accounts, Attorney General, and Secretary of State each appoint one member. All are subject to Senate confirmation. The Registry is responsible for receiving campaign finance reports from candidates and making them available for public inspection. In fact, much of the reasoning behind the twenty-eight-day period discussed in the preceding paragraph was to help insure public knowledge of contribution patterns before an election. The Registry is also required to issue summary reports after an election. It has the authority to conduct random audits of campaign committees and to use civil action to try and enforce many of the provisions of the campaign finance law. The Registry has the authority to initiate investigations, including the use of subpoena power, and forwards to the Attorney General any violations that might result in civil or criminal prosecution.[12]

Probably the most significant change resulting from the 1992 legislation, however, was the creation of a public financing system for gubernatorial elections and associated expenditure limits. The law established initial *voluntary* expenditure limits of $1.8 million for the primary and $1.8 million for the general election. The limits are adjusted by the consumer price index before each gubernatorial election to take into account inflationary effects in the economy. The law encourages acceptance of the expenditure limits by providing pubic campaign subsidies only to those candidates who agree to abide by the expenditure limits. Once a candidate achieves a minimum threshold of $300,000 in private contributions and agrees to abide by the expenditure limits, the state then matches each private contribution at a rate of 2 to 1 to a maximum state subsidy of $1.2 million.[13] As a further incentive to induce *all* candidates to abide by the voluntary expenditure limits, if any one candidate in an election exceeds the limit, all other candidates in the election are allowed to exceed the expenditure limit while continuing to receive matching funds. If a candidate refuses public funds in the primary, he or she cannot receive public funds in the general election. And if a candidate accepts public funds in the primary, he or she must utilize the public subsidy in the general election and abide by the expenditure limit. A final critical component of the law is a requirement that each candidate receiving public funds must participate in publicly televised debates, with the maximum number of debates set at six.

Prior to the adoption of the 1992 reform act, Republicans were consistently underfunded relative to their Democratic opponents. In the general elections of 1979, 1983, 1987, and 1991, Republican gubernatorial candidates spent $1,225,148, $1,364,700, $263,459, and $1,813,362, respectively. The equivalent figures for Democratic Party candidates were $1,863,250, $1,559,510, $3,141,463, and $3,426,948. In every case the Democratic candidate was able to outspend his or her Republican opponent. Only in 1983 was the Republican candidate able to come within $200,000 of his Democratic opponent. Notably, the 1983 election was also the most competitive of these four elections in that the Democrat received "only" 55 percent of the vote in the general election. The Democrats got

59 percent of the vote in 1979 and 65 percent of the vote in 1987 and 1991. Although voter turnout reached nearly 40 percent of the voting age population in 1983, it had dropped to near 30 percent for the elections of 1987 and 1991.

The 1995 gubernatorial election was the first election operating under the provisions of the new campaign finance act. Because of a state constitutional amendment, it was also the first gubernatorial election in over a hundred years where the winning candidate would actually be able to run for reelection.[14] Results of the 1995 election seemed to support the rhetoric of those who had fought for the passage of the campaign reform act. All major candidates agreed to abide by the new expenditure limits. The Democratic primary had four candidates, with the winning candidate receiving about 44 percent of the vote and two other candidates each receiving over 20 percent. Over $6.7 million dollars was spent by all of the candidates in both primaries. In the general election, each of the major candidates spent approximately $1.8 million, with the Republican slightly outspending the Democratic candidate. The level playing field in terms of campaign finances appeared to spur a heavily contested election. Polls immediately before the election indicated a dead-even race and Republicans went into the last weekend feeling confident. The Democratic candidate won, but with slightly less than 51 percent of the vote, a victory margin of less than 21,400 votes out of almost 980,000 votes cast.

Proponents of the campaign finance law felt vindicated. Individual candidate expenditures were reduced from what had been spent in recent gubernatorial elections, and yet the Democratic primary remained competitive. Further, the ability of serious candidates to raise sufficient funds in order to reach the minimum threshold for matching funds minimized fears that the $500 contribution limit might make it difficult for candidates to raise money. While voter turnout was a little over 30 percent of the voting age population in 1987 and 1991, it reached over 35 percent in 1995, perhaps because the election was the most competitive gubernatorial election in Kentucky in nearly three decades. From the perspective of its supporters, the campaign finance law had worked: candidates were able to raise sufficient funds to run a viable campaign; total expenditures had been reduced; candidates now had equal financial opportunities; voter turnout had been increased; and, most importantly, voters were given a competitive election.

As the 1999 gubernatorial election approached, growing Republican strength in the state of Kentucky was evident. After the 1998 congressional elections, both of Kentucky's U.S. senators and five of the state's six congressional representatives were Republicans. And, as stated above, in the summer of 1999, Republicans took control of the Kentucky Senate when two state senators switched parties. With the state increasingly tilted toward the Republican Party and a public financing system that allowed for greater fundraising parity, the

1999 election seemed the ideal setting for Republicans to make a strong run at the governor's office. Standing in the way of a possible Republican victory, however, was incumbent Governor Paul Patton, the first Kentucky governor able to run for reelection in over one hundred years.

With a popular incumbent governor running for reelection, almost every aspect of the campaign finance law that seemed to work so well in 1995 proved to be a failure in 1999. No major figure in the Republican Party sought the nomination for governor. The eventual Republican nominee, publicist Peppy Martin, received only minimal help from the Republican Party. Kentucky's senior U.S. senator and major national fundraiser, Mitch McConnell, refused to endorse her and was generally seen as hostile to her candidacy. As the election approached, the only question of interest was whether or not the Republican candidate would end up in third place behind Reform Party candidate Gatewood Gailbraith, a candidate notable largely for advocating the legalization of hemp.

In the general election the Democratic incumbent received more than 61 percent of the vote, while his Republican challenger finished a distant second with just over 22 percent of the vote. Only about 22 percent of the voting age population turned out to vote. No candidate received public funding for the 1999 gubernatorial election. According to Kentucky's campaign finance law, at least two candidates must meet the minimum threshold level of $300,000 before any candidate can receive public funds. Only the incumbent governor ever met this threshold, spending approximately one million dollars in the fall campaign. Both the Republican candidate and the Reform Party candidate spent less than $50,000 in the general election. Thus, unlike the 1995 gubernatorial election, the election of 1999 was again characterized by a candidate with a massive financial advantage—this time a powerful incumbent opposed by two underfunded opponents—resulting in an uncompetitive, low voter turnout election.

What happened in 1999? Critics of the campaign finance reform law argue that its provisions made it too difficult for an opposition candidate to raise sufficient funds to seriously challenge an incumbent governor. The expenditure limits, they reason, were too low for a challenger to mount a credible campaign. As a result, no major Republican candidate chose to run for governor in 1999. Supporters of campaign finance reform contend that while financial considerations were a component of the campaign in 1999, financial considerations were secondary to other factors, the most important being a popular incumbent running for reelection. Disputes within the Republican Party after Martin won the nomination only made a bad situation worse. In this sense, Republican decisions made long before the primary helped insure the reelection of Governor Patton in an uncompetitive, low turnout election. Had the 1992 campaign finance law not been in force, reformers contend, little would have changed in how the 1999 election developed.

Perhaps what the two Kentucky elections and the Jesse Ventura election in Minnesota best illustrate, however, is the inherent problem in trying to evaluate the consequences of campaign finance reform with a limited set of elections or within a single electoral context. Anecdotal evidence may make for good story telling, but it hardly provides the basis for broad generalizations regarding the electoral consequences of reform. Clearly, a more comprehensive approach is needed.

## EVALUATING CAMPAIGN FINANCE REFORM

Over the past several decades much has been written about the ways candidates raise and spend money. Yet, despite an impressive body of literature, we can say very little with certainty about the electoral consequences of campaign finance laws. In part, this uncertainty reflects the fact that, at least since 1974, much of the research on campaign finance has focused on U.S. national elections.[15] Though the system of campaign finance has proven to be highly malleable (the Federal Election Campaign Act was amended in 1976 and 1979), the statutes governing federal campaign fundraising have, until 2002, remained relatively constant. Therefore, our understanding of the electoral consequences of campaign finance laws at the national level is largely (though not entirely) limited to a single regulatory regime—the Federal Election Campaign Act of 1971 and its subsequent amendments.

Works evaluating campaign finance at the state level have more regimes to analyze, but nevertheless were limited in scope. First, most of the earlier works focused on either a single state or limited number of states and a limited time frame.[16] More recent studies have expanded the scope of the analysis and provided considerable insight into the "lost world" of state-level campaign finance,[17] but have also been limited in terms of their ability to provide a comprehensive assessment of state reform efforts. For example, writing the conclusions for the most exhaustive study of state legislative campaign finance to date, Malcolm Jewell and William Cassie observe that there is not enough evidence "to conclude that public financing would succeed or fail in meeting the goals of reformers."[18] In his analysis, Robert Hogan concludes that while campaign finance laws have a statistically significant impact on campaign spending in state legislative elections, the impact is relatively modest compared to other factors. Along these lines, Hogan finds that both contribution limits and public funding reduce campaign spending, but that "these effects are limited primarily to incumbents."[19]

Second, most of what we know about campaign finance has been derived from work on campaign spending in legislative elections,[20] the findings of which may or may not be applicable to gubernatorial campaigns.[21] Looking at the effects of candidate spending on electoral outcomes, Randall Partin found that gubernatorial elections are "a horse race of a different color" in that, unlike legislative elections, incumbent spending matters almost as much as challenger spending.[22] In addition, gubernatorial elections are more visible; generate greater media coverage; attract more experienced, better funded opposition candidates; and are generally more competitive than legislative elections.[23] As such, campaign finance reforms may have a much different effect on gubernatorial than on legislative campaigns.

As this brief review of the literature illustrates, works on campaign finance reform have developed into two often separate strands. Literature focusing on campaign finance at the national level has been methodologically sophisticated, but suffers from limited variance in campaign finance laws. The state-level literature, which has the potential to say much more about the electoral consequences of campaign finance laws, has tended to be limited in scope because of practical limitations in data collection.[24] Therefore, generalizations about the consequences of state campaign finance regulations are often limited as well.

This book attempts to overcome the limitations of the separate literature strands by focusing on the impact of campaign finance laws on candidate spending, voter turnout, electoral competition, and electoral outcomes in gubernatorial elections. We improve on prior work in several ways: First, utilizing data on gubernatorial elections, we are able to account for the variance in state campaign finance laws across all fifty states, and to do so over a considerable time frame (1978–97).[25] Because state legislatures have been more willing to impose reform on gubernatorial candidates than on themselves, there is considerably more variance in public financing schemes (and spending limits) for gubernatorial elections than for state legislative elections. Second, by paying greater attention to the measurement of state reform efforts we are better able to distinguish between the effects of contribution limits, spending limits, and public financing on the electoral process. Third, with these improved measures of the state legal framework, we are able to make stronger, more convincing inferences regarding the effects of campaign finance reform on candidate spending, voter turnout, electoral competition, and electoral outcomes.

We begin in chapter 1 by providing a brief history of campaign finance reform at the state level, beginning with Maryland's effort to regulate the use of liquor to buy votes and continuing through the recent wave of "clean money" initiatives. In chapter 2, we consider some of the arguments made for and against specific reform provisions (contribution limits, spending limits, and public financing). Though reform is often discussed as though it were a singular measure, it is, in reality, a patchwork of different measures, each with a different intent and set of consequences. In chapter 3, we outline patterns of spending in gubernatorial elections. How has spending increased over time? What are the patterns of spending across the states? We examine the importance of population size, geographic size, and economic well-being to the evolution of spending patterns. Finally, spending in gubernatorial elections is compared to spending in House (aggregated by state) and Senate elections. In chapter 4, we expand this analysis to look more specifically at the impact of state campaign finance laws on candidate spending. In this respect, we examine the measurable impact of contribution limits, spending limits, and public financing on candidate campaign spending in gubernatorial elections.

In chapter 5, we examine patterns of electoral competition in gubernatorial elections, and then investigate whether these patterns of competition are related, either directly or indirectly, to state campaign finance laws. In chapter 6, we analyze whether, and how, campaign finance laws affect electoral outcomes. In particular, we evaluate how contribution limits, spending limits, and public financing affect the "incumbency advantage" and the partisanship of electoral outcomes. In chapter 7, we turn our attention to voter turnout and, in particular, to the question of whether patterns of voter turnout are related to state campaign finance laws. Finally, in chapter 8, we summarize the major findings of the text, provide an analysis of some recent campaign reform efforts, and offer suggestions for effective campaign finance reform.

# CHAPTER 1

# A History of State Campaign Finance Reform

After more than twenty-five years of debate, the nation began the new millennium without a resolution to *the* major issue of governmental reform in the last quarter of the twentieth century: campaign finance.[1] As John McCain and Bill Bradley made campaign finance reform the centerpiece of their insurgent campaigns for the presidency in the year 2000, the 106th Congress began with continued congressional stalemate over the direction of reform efforts. The collapse of the energy giant Enron and the growing specter of a major political and financial scandal, however, prompted Congress to act. President Bush, in the spring of 2002, signed into law McCain–Feingold, which attempted to address what many considered the most egregious problem in contemporary campaign finance: soft money. While these developments helped assure that campaign finance reform would remain part of the national consciousness, they also helped reinforce an all too common focus on national-level reforms.[2] It is often forgotten that states have the prime responsibility for establishing the rules and regulations, including campaign finance regulations, that govern most elections in the United States.[3]

As we discussed in the introduction, the analysis of gubernatorial elections affords one a number of unique opportunities in which to analyze the effects of campaign finance reform legislation. All states operate within similar constitutional structures and all have been affected by similar nationwide trends in gubernatorial campaigns towards more expensive candidate-centered elections.[4] At the same time, states differ a good deal in the nature of their campaign finance laws, and a number of states have made significant changes in their campaign finance laws over the last twenty-five years. This variation in campaign finance regulations allows one to examine the effects of these regulations in a way that is simply not possible at the federal level where the basic statutes remained unchanged for over twenty-five years until the recent passage of the McCain–Feingold legislation.

This chapter provides a starting point for our investigation. It begins with a brief historical overview of the evolution of state campaign finance regulations prior to the post–Watergate reform era. Next, we discuss developments in two major categories of reform in the post–Watergate era. In particular, we examine how states have adopted certain of these reforms over the time series we are analyzing, 1978 to 1998, and the current status of reform efforts in the states.

## STATE CAMPAIGN FINANCE REGULATIONS
## IN THE PRE–WATERGATE ERA

Despite the recent attention on federal campaign finance laws, the regulation of the use of money in most elections in the United States, including gubernatorial elections, has always been largely a state function. There is no doubt that, throughout the history of the United States, money has been a central component of most election campaigns.[5] At the same time, it has only been during the last thirty to forty years that campaign finance itself has become the focus of significant and comprehensive state reform efforts. Prior to the 1970s, reform efforts tended to focus on specific practices, such as vote buying, that were perceived to be inappropriate or corrupt.[6] Consequently, state campaign finance laws tended to be patchwork responses to scandals and publicity associated with specific campaign practices.

Regulations aimed at stopping bribery and other types of enticements for voting were the first type of campaign finance regulations passed by the states. In the earliest years of the Republic, liquor was often used to win voter loyalty.[7] As the practice fell into disrepute, Maryland passed legislation in 1811 that prohibited passing out liquor to voters. Other states soon followed. Most states prohibited (and continue to prohibit) bribery either in their constitution or in statutes. However, the definition of bribery, or what some might call indirect forms of bribery, continued to be problematic as candidates and their advisors sought new methods to gather votes and states responded with new statutory prohibitions. A number of states eventually would prohibit betting on elections, providing liquor or tobacco as an enticement for voting, paying naturalization fees as a way to influence voters, and transporting voters to the polls, as well as restricting the number of individuals that could be hired as poll watchers. Even today, while all states prohibit vote buying, there is a great deal of difference among the states in the degree to which certain types of practices, which some view as indirect forms of bribery, are limited or prohibited.[8]

## Contribution Limits

As the nation began to change, states were forced to confront a number of political practices that would become the focus of further reform efforts. The development of mass-based parties and the expansion of the electorate in the first part of the nineteenth century forever changed the nature of campaigns and elections in America. As more voters needed to be contacted and party organizational efforts became an essential part of political campaigns, campaign expenses began to expand. No longer could candidates finance much of their own campaigns. A source for funds was needed and patronage provided a natural reservoir. Government employees were simply required to "donate" part of their paycheck to the political party.[9] Patronage and the spoils system became a major source of revenue for candidates and political parties and a major source of corruption. It was in response to this system and its associated corruption that a number of states began to institute a variety of finance reforms at the end of the nineteenth century.

The last half of the nineteenth century was one of the most politically corrupt periods in all of American history. Overt corruption at all levels of government led to calls for reform. In 1876, Rutherford B. Hayes ran for president on a platform that called for civil service reform. It was not until 1883, however, that the Civil Service Reform Act was passed by Congress and signed into law by President Chester Arthur. Similar laws were soon passed by a number of states. New York took the lead when it passed its own Civil Service Reform Act in 1883. Individuals could no longer solicit campaign contributions in public buildings, and public employees were protected from having political assessments as a requirement for employment. Massachusetts and Pennsylvania soon passed similar laws.[10] By 1966, nineteen states had laws that limited or prohibited the collection of campaign funds from governmental employees or restricted campaign activities in governmental buildings.[11] In 2002, forty-five states had such laws.

These laws prohibiting the assessment of public employees were the first major attempt by states to regulate campaign contributions; but they would not be the last. At the end of the nineteenth century, corporate contributions to political parties and candidates had become a common way of financing campaigns.[12] So as the spoils system came under increasing attack, candidates and political parties began to have a greater reliance upon corporations and wealthy individuals as a source for campaign monies. But, much as the public mood had soured on the system of assessments, the public began to have an ever-more cynical attitude toward business and government as written accounts of political abuses at the federal, state, and local levels became more commonplace.[13] States began to act; by 1905, five had placed a prohibition on contributions from corporations.[14] In 1907, Congress passed the Tillman Act prohibiting corporations and banks from contributing funds to candidates for national office. As of 1932, thirty-four states prohibited corporate contributions.[15]

Other limits on contributions would be passed into federal and state law. By 1941, Republican concerns over the growing presence of union money in the Democratic Party led to a temporary ban on labor union contributions to national political organizations. Four years later, the Taft–Hartley Act made the ban permanent and extended it to include expenditures on behalf of a candidate. A number of states followed this lead so that by the early 1960s, five states prohibited labor union contributions to political candidates.

Numerous states would ban anonymous contributions, contributions by one person in the name of another person, and cash contributions over a given amount of money, $100, for example. By 1932, two states had laws that placed limits on the size of contributions from individuals, with the number rising to seven by 1962.[16] Because PAC contributions are a post–World War II development and were not a significant factor in most gubernatorial elections until the 1970s, state regulation of PAC contributions was not a major consideration in most states until the post–Watergate era.[17]

## Expenditure Limits

Although states eventually began to place restrictions on contributions, throughout the history of the United States there has generally been a greater focus on the control of expenditures. As suggested earlier, this control is very much the result of the tendency of reformers to focus on specific activities and the need to prohibit or limit such activities. The clearest example of this tendency has already been discussed: attempts to eliminate bribery and voter enticements. For example, if you do not want liquor to be used to entice voters to act in a particular manner, then the reasonable thing to do is to prohibit candidates from spending money on such an activity. All states would eventually place some prohibitions on the expenditure of campaign monies.

While limits on specific types of expenditures were the first and most widespread examples of federal and state attempts to control expenditures, calls for reform in the first part of the twentieth century began to zero in controlling total expenditures. Federal legislation in 1911 and 1925 placed campaign expenditure limits on House and Senate elections.[18] States, whose laws typically applied only to gubernatorial and other statewide elections, also initiated efforts to control total expenditures and contributions so that by 1932 over half of the states had such provisions. By 1964, thirty states had provisions that attempted, in one way or another, to limit total campaign expenditures.

These state laws that attempted to limit campaign expenditures differed in a number of important respects. Most of the laws applied to gubernatorial and other statewide elections, but some also applied to U.S. House and Senate elections. Some states exempted certain types of expenditures, such as filing fees, postage, printing costs, and advertising. In some states expenditure limits applied only to primary elections, while in other states only to the general elections. In some states there were separate limits for the primary and the general elections, while in others there was a single limit for all primary and general election spending. A number of states explicitly listed legitimate expenditures. States also differed in terms of whom the limits applied to. In some states expenditure limits applied only to candidates, while in others the limits also applied to committees operating on behalf of a candidate.[19] In addition, enforcement provisions and the consequences associated with violation of the laws differed greatly among the states.

Most indications suggest that the various pre-1970 expenditure limit laws were not very successful in achieving their goals.[20] In a number of cases, the laws suffered from too many exemptions or did not clearly specify the responsibilities of the numerous individuals and groups involved in a campaign. Many laws also lacked effective enforcement mechanisms, a deficiency made even more problematic by politicos who lacked much incentive to press for enforcement once the initial public calls for reform began to drift into the distant past. Finally, much as we see today, expenditures made on behalf of a candidate became increasingly difficult to specify and control.

## Public Financing

Contemporary calls for reform of the campaign finance system often involve proposals to regulate contributions and expenditures and proposals for the public financing of candidates for office. While attempts to regulate contributions and expenditures had been tried in the past, prior to the 1970s, state efforts to provide public funding to campaigns had been minimal to nonexistent. At the beginning of the twentieth century, a few states began the practice of distributing, at state expense, official bulletins in which each candidate was given some space to present a campaign message.[21] By 1966, only Oregon continued the practice. At times, states have also spent money to advertise lists of candidates in the newspaper, provide sample ballots to voters, and provide services on educational television.[22] Beyond such minimalist efforts, however, prior to the 1970s, Colorado was the only state to experiment with a significant direct subsidy for campaign efforts. In 1909, the Colorado legislature passed legislation that gave each political party a sum of money from the state treasury equal to twenty-five cents for each vote cast for the party's gubernatorial candidate at the last general election. The money was to be used to help cover campaign expenses. The law was quickly declared unconstitutional by the Colorado Supreme Court and then repealed by the state legislature. It would take until the late 1960s and early 1970s before the idea of using state expenditures to help finance campaigns would again receive serious consideration.

## Publicity

The history of state efforts to regulate campaign financing is generally a history of disjointed efforts in response to scandals and publicity associated with specific campaign practices. However, if there is one unifying principle that has been associated with almost all reform efforts, even those being undertaken today, it is the perspective that public awareness or publicity (record keeping and public disclosure) is the cornerstone of reform. This perspective reflects an abiding faith in the ability of an informed citizenry to be the ultimate judge of campaign financial behaviors.

In 1890, New York passed the first publicity law in the United States. It was soon followed by laws in six additional states: Colorado, Michigan, Massachusetts, California, Missouri, and Kansas.[23] By 1905, fourteen states had publicity laws, and the number increased to forty-five by 1932. Despite their rapid spread throughout the United States in the first part of the twentieth century, publicity laws differed in terms of who or what organizations were required to file reports, the contents of reports, timing of report submission, who received the reports, enforcement provisions, and procedures for public disclosure. Some states only required candidates to file reports, while others extended reporting requirements to all political committees. In a limited number of cases, the states required reports from all organizations or individuals who actively supported or opposed a candidate. All expenditures and contributions generally had to be reported, but the amount of detail differed among the states. As is the case today, the secretary of state was typically the individual assigned to receive reports. However, in some cases there was no central depository for campaign reports. Penalties for violating the publicity laws were generally minimal and most states simply had no provisions for auditing reports or making referrals for prosecution.

In many respects, the most problematic aspects of these early publicity laws relate to their timing provisions and their procedures for public disclosure. In most of the states, reports were filed after the primary or general election. Only seventeen states required reports to be filed before the election. All states kept the reports and had them open for public inspection, but in almost all cases there was no official publication of the records nor were there any analyses of the reports.[24] If citizens wanted campaign finance information, they had to depend upon candidates, newspaper reports, or their own initiative.

The publicity laws passed in the first half of the twentieth century were not very effective. After the initial wave of reform, there was little incentive for compliance or enforcement. Candidates and other political organizations often simply did not file reports. Enforcement provisions, often minimal to begin with, received little attention from political officials. And while a democratic faith in an informed citizenry formed the foundation for publicity laws, citizens rarely obtained useful information in a timely manner. As one can see in this brief historical overview of campaign finance reform efforts in the pre–Watergate era, many of the proposals for reform that have been put forward in the post–Watergate era have been tried in some fashion, in some state, throughout our nation's history: reporting and disclosure requirements (publicity), limits on campaign contributions, limits on expenditures, and public funding for campaign activities. However, because most of these laws developed in response to scandals and publicity associated with specific campaign practices, the overall system of campaign finance itself rarely became an issue.[25] Thus, comprehensive campaign finance reform as a sustained political issue never developed in the states. In this respect, the Watergate scandal of 1972–73 can be seen as the single most important event in the history of comprehensive campaign finance reform. Since that event, the overall system of campaign finance and comprehensive reform has been at the center of public debate at both the national and state levels. No longer do reformers simply focus on specific campaign activities that need to be modified or eliminated; rather the entire system of financing elections has become the subject of debate.

## STATE CAMPAIGN FINANCE REFORM EFFORTS
## IN THE POST–WATERGATE ERA

The Watergate scandal focused the nation's attention on the issue of campaign finance reform to a degree never seen before in America's history. While most previous reform efforts at the national and state level arose and focused on specific campaign practices, Watergate brought into question the entire system of campaign finance in America. Watergate ushered in the era of campaign finance reform debate that has now been going on for over thirty years. During this period, approximately two-thirds of the states have passed campaign finance reforms that have differed in degree of complexity and purpose, and reform efforts continue to evolve in response to federal legislation, U.S. Supreme Court decisions, state Supreme Court decisions, experience with reform proposals, and new perspectives on the goals of reform.

As in the past, publicity remained a cornerstone of all state reform efforts. While forty-five states had some form of reporting and disclosure requirements in 1970, today all fifty states have such requirements. In addition, numerous states have reformed their reporting and disclosure requirements to provide more information on candidate campaigns, to speed up their reporting time, and to extend coverage to more noncandidate organizations and individuals.[26] And it seems likely that states will have to continue to modify their reporting and disclosure requirements in response to new ways being used to circumvent current laws, such as Internet technology.[27]

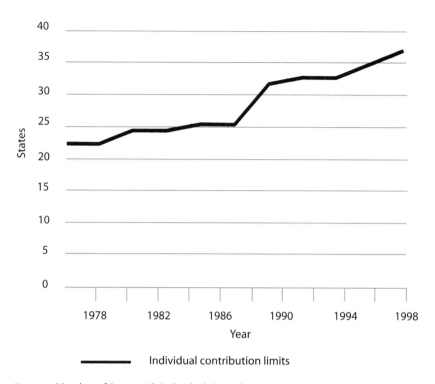

**Figure 1.1** Number of States with Individual Contribution Limits, 1978–98

Probably the most common change in state campaign finance laws over the last twenty-five years has been the imposition of more stringent contribution limits. Soon after the imposition of federal legislation in 1976 that placed limits on the size of contributions by individuals to candidates for federal office, approximately twenty states followed suit. Figure 1.1 shows the number of states that had limits on individual contributions to gubernatorial campaigns for every other year from 1978 to 1998. As can be seen, the number grew from twenty-two in 1978 to thirty-one by 1990 and thirty-six in 1998.

Figure 1.2 portrays the growth in the number of states limiting contributions to gubernatorial campaigns by corporations, unions, and PACs. As was the case with limits on individual contributions, limits imposed by states on contributions from organizations surged in the 1990s. By 1998, forty-three states had imposed limits on corporate contributions, while forty-two states and thirty-seven states had imposed limits on contributions by unions and PACs, respectively. In addition, twenty-two states actually ban corporate contributions to gubernatorial campaigns, while thirteen ban labor union contributions.[28]

As suggested by Michael Malbin and Thomas Gais, the movement towards greater restrictions on contributions in the late 1980s and most of the 1990s

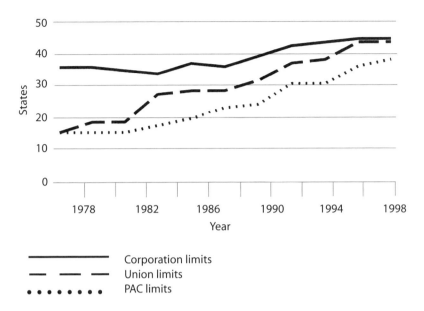

**Figure 1.2** Number of States with Corporation, Union, and PAC Contribution Limits, 1978–98

reflected a change in the objectives of campaign finance reform.[29] The laws in the early to mid-1970s often focused on reducing the role of the "fat cat" contributor and other "big time" players. The intent of these early laws was to prevent extreme questionable behaviors that the public perceived as linked to corruption and inappropriate influence. By 1980, thirty-five states placed limits on corporate contributions in response to traditional suspicions associated with corporate giving.

During the 1990s, thinking about comprehensive campaign finance reform shifted towards equalizing political power. Of special concern was that "special interests" that contributed to campaigns gained an unfair advantage in the political process. Thus, three additional goals became the focus of reform efforts: reduce the cost of elections; significantly reduce the importance of *any* single contributor by keeping contribution limits low; and force candidates to rely upon a large number of contributions so that any potential influence resulting from contributions is as widely dispersed as possible. This focus on equity helped push the reform movement throughout the 1990s as more and more states added contribution limits to cover more and more individuals and organizations. Of equal importance was the move, in a number of states, to reduce the size of contribution limits that were already in place.[30]

If publicity and contribution limits were two critical components of comprehensive campaign finance reform in the post–Watergate era, spending limits

**9**

and the public financing of gubernatorial elections are the third component. As will be seen shortly, while public financing of elections and spending limits are two different mechanisms designed to reform state campaign finance systems, in actual practice they are usually closely linked.

There are basically two alternative types of public financing of campaigns used in the states. One alternative is to provide money to political parties; the second alternative is to provide money to candidates.[31] The goals of the two public financing systems can be quite different and somewhat at odds with each other.

Party-based public funding systems are based on the view that political parties are central to the democratic/electoral process in the United States. According to this perspective, political parties are to be maintained and/or strengthened in order to fulfill their responsibilities as linkage mechanisms among candidates, citizens, and voters. As such, there are three possible benefits that can result from a stronger financial role for political parties. First, political parties represent an aggregate of a large number of interests and, therefore, have a broad overarching view of the public good. This representation of multiple interests is seen as preferable to the narrow self-interested viewpoint of contributors such as PACs and interest groups. Second, political parties often play a central role in grassroots "get-out-the-vote" efforts and, therefore, given greater financial resources, party efforts ought to result in increased voter turnout. Finally, public financing of political parties is seen as a potential source of increased electoral competition. American political parties have a fundamental concern with winning elections. Given this focus, they are not likely to waste money on elections in which they have little chance to win or which they are certain to win; rather, they will allocate money strategically in order to maximize their total number of electoral victories. The net effect of this strategic behavior is an increased number of competitive elections.[32]

Public subsidies to candidates place a greater emphasis on elections as contests among individuals. In this context, political parties are often viewed with skepticism, as being part of the twin problems of corruption and influence peddling, and, especially at the national level, as mechanisms for avoiding reforms of the financing system. Public subsidies to candidates, whether in the form of direct grants or matching funds, are seen as a way to minimize the undue influence and corruption often ascribed to contributors and partisan fundraising. Because public funding reduces the specter of corruption, it should help to restore trust in democratic processes. In addition, publicly financed elections ensure that both candidates, but most importantly challengers, have sufficient funds to run a serious campaign. Where both candidates have enough money to run serious campaigns, elections, especially those where the spending is relatively equal, will be more competitive. A third goal of public financing is higher voter turnout. We know that more competitive elections tend to have higher voter turnout. Thus, if public financing makes elections more competitive, higher voter turnout should follow. Finally, public financing of candidates is often used as a way to induce candidates to accept spending limits.

Spending, or expenditure, limits are a mechanism that is often proposed to limit what some view as the ever-escalating cost of elections in the United States and the resulting need to generate more and more money from contributors. In this sense, especially in combination with contribution limits, spending limits are seen as a way to reduce the power of large contributors. Proponents also argue that spending limits are likely to reduce the disparity in spending between candidates that we often see in American elections and, in many cases, may actually equalize it.[33] The result of such equalization would be increased electoral competition and voter turnout.

In 1976, the U.S. Supreme Court put forward its decision in the case of *Buckley v. Valeo,* which challenged a number of the provisions of the 1974 amendments to the Federal Election Campaign Act.[34] In many respects, this decision represents the single greatest impediment to comprehensive campaign finance regulation.[35] In its decision the Supreme Court ruled that spending is a form of free speech. Attempts to limit spending, without some accompanying form of public financing, violates First Amendment protections of freedom of expression. As such, to pass constitutional muster, spending limits must be voluntary, though candidates abiding by the spending limits can be provided public subsidies to encourage their acceptance of the limits.

The *Buckley* decision made it clear that states could not simply pass mandatory spending limits.[36] Proponents of reform in the states, therefore, turned to the federal model of using public subsidies to encourage presidential candidates to accept spending limits as they began to design proposals for their state's campaign finance reform system. Today, the norm among states with public financing of elections or campaign spending limits is to link the two. As of 1998, fourteen states, up from only seven in 1980, had some type of public financing provision for gubernatorial candidates, and in thirteen of those states expenditure limits were a condition for receiving public funds.[37] Three states had expenditure limits that were neither mandatory nor tied to the acceptance of public funds; the limits are in essence recommendations with minimal force of law. In this sense, while conceptually distinct, public financing of candidates and expenditure limits have become a singular linked characteristic of the post–Watergate reform efforts.

## CONCLUSIONS

As can be seen by this brief historical overview of campaign finance reform, states have often fulfilled their role as "laboratories of democracy." States, and their local and federal counterparts, have attempted to regulate campaign finance by developing a patchwork of regulations in response to particular political situations. Regulation attempts increased greatly after the Watergate scandal brought problems attendant with campaign financing to the forefront and compelled the national and state governments to focus their attention on a wide range of issues and reform proposals. As we write this text, states continue to modify and expand finance reform efforts, providing natural laboratories in which to analyze the effects of various reform efforts.

It is this opportunity to evaluate the effects of alternative reform proposals in the context of gubernatorial elections that is the focus of the rest of this book. In the next chapter, we lay out the debates over the consequences of reform. These debates will help specify the issues that we will evaluate, using empirical analysis, in the subsequent chapters of this text.

# CHAPTER 2

## The Rhetoric of Reform

Though often discussed as an aggregate, campaign finance reform is in reality a collection of smaller measures each with a different intent and set of likely consequences. The potential combinations of these various measures (contribution limits, public funding, spending limits, disclosure requirements) into comprehensive reform packages are virtually limitless—as are the potential consequences of these various reforms. Despite the variety of reform options and potential consequences, the temptation to overgeneralize about the electoral consequences of reform is rarely resisted by either the supporters or opponents of reform.

For supporters, reform reinvigorates democratic governance. By leveling the playing field in campaign fundraising, reform increases electoral competition. By reducing the influence of large contributors, it returns political power to John and Jane Q. Public, thus stimulating voter turnout and electoral participation. For opponents, the effects of reform are no less substantial, though the consequences are considerably direr. By placing limits on contributions and expenditures, reform muzzles political expression and participation. By limiting challenger spending, reform protects incumbents, thereby eroding electoral competition. In short, depending on one's point of view, reform is a panacea, a colossal failure, or a threat to the functioning of democratic governance.

Nor is the rhetoric of reform limited to potential consequences; it extends to the advocates and opponents of reform as well. Opponents of reform often portray advocates as good-natured simpletons operating under positive intentions but hopelessly naive when it comes to "real" politics. Frank Sorauf, for example, writes:

If there is any constant in the confusions about American campaign finance in the twentieth century, it is in the repeated attempts to reform it to rely on the small sums of ordinary citizens. The history of those attempts is not a happy one, and yet we have not given up. American optimism about the efficacy of reform, ironically, has run as deep as American distrust of the cash we have tried vainly to reform. So the reformers have persisted throughout the century, their efforts often limited to half-measures and just as often greeted with knowing winks.[1]

According to this particular portrayal, reformers are Progressive/Populist do-gooders, motivated by a "cynical innocence" leading them to distrust the power and influence of money, even as they embrace the possibilities of reform.[2] Not all accounts of reformers are so kind. Bradley Smith contends that more cynical motives underlie reform efforts. As Smith observes:

> Campaign reform is usually sold as a populist means to strengthen the power of "ordinary" citizens against dominant, big money interests. In fact, campaign finance reform has favored selected elites and further isolated individuals from the political process.[3]

For Smith, media elites, labor unions, political consulting firms, and political activists all benefit from reform—even though these groups "may or may not be more representative of public opinion than the wealthy philanthropists and industrialists who financed so many past campaigns."[4]

The rhetoric of opponents is matched or exceeded by those groups supporting reform. Consider, for example, the following account of Mitch McConnell's opposition to campaign finance reform on First Amendment grounds:

> The truth is Mitch McConnell is no First Amendment avenger. Except when it comes to wrapping legalized bribery in the mantle of free speech, he has eagerly seized nearly every opportunity from regulating the Internet to banning flag-burning to use the power of the government to silence unpopular speech. Yet, ever so masterfully, he framed the debate over McCain–Feingold with a false passion for speech, coupled with a convincing, though ultimately illusory, pretense at First Amendment expertise. His success in characterizing all campaign finance reform as an attack on the First Amendment should go down in history as one of the great triumphs of Orwellian double-speak. . . . The truth is, Senator McConnell's First Amendment applies only to the wealthy special interests who finance campaigns.[5]

Though most reform rhetoric has been aimed at Republicans, and in particular at Mitch McConnell, Democrats have also been targeted for hypocrisy in superficially supporting reform, even while working behind the scenes to ensure that reform would never be enacted. As Elizabeth Drew describes it: "A member would declare support for reform, but manage not to have to actually vote for it if there was any real danger that a substantial bill would be enacted into law. Thus, people could vote for a bill they knew a president would veto, or that they assumed that the other chamber wouldn't pass, and still claim credit as a backer of reform."[6] The result is discussion of reform that never quite makes it into law, even as most public officials claim to support reform. Consider, for example, Drew's account of the 1997 debate over the McCain–Feingold campaign finance proposal: "[M]ost elected politicians, whatever their rhetoric, don't favor giving challengers a level playing field. And one by one, the provisions that would have done that were eliminated from McCain's bill even before it went to the Senate floor."[7]

The intractability of national politics, and cynicism about what might emerge under the label of "reform," led reform groups to turn to the states, where resistance (though considerable) is often less well entrenched. The most visible of these efforts has been the Ellen Miller-led Public Campaign that advocates Clean Money Campaign Reform (CMCR), a combination of spending limits, public financing, and free media time. Where state legislatures have resisted the reformist impulse, reformers have made use of the levers of direct democracy (the referendum and initiative)—at least in those states where these levers are available. Yet, successfully passing campaign reform is hardly an assurance that campaign finance reform will work, or for that matter that it will even be implemented.

First, wherever reform is enacted, a court case is sure to follow. While reform groups have worked to help write laws that they believe will pass constitutional muster, the guiding precedent (*Buckley v. Valeo*) has been subjected to widely different interpretations—as well as considerable criticism. In fact, both reformers and opponents would like to see *Buckley* overturned but for fundamentally different reasons. Reformers would like the court to reconsider the constitutional viability of spending limits,[8] while opponents would like to see *Buckley*'s First Amendment logic extended to cover contribution limits. Given this context, the courts are likely to weigh in on any change in state or local campaign finance laws. While Maine's Clean Election Law has withstood at least one challenge in federal court, recently passed laws in Vermont and Arizona remain under challenge.

Second, even where initiatives are used to pass reform, public officials can still thwart implementation. The most glaring example has been in Massachusetts, where the Massachusetts State Assembly has resisted funding the public funding mechanisms passed by a 2–1 margin by voters in 1998. As a *Boston Globe* report described it:

> In the wee hours of the morning with no debate, House leaders pushed through a measure Friday that would erode a key part of anticorruption laws and allow special interests to wine and dine lawmakers without reporting much of the expense. . . . House members also quietly attached a rider that would suspend the state's so-called clean elections law, which would publicly fund state elections.[9]

What is perhaps most notable about the resistance is that it has come from Democratic leaders, some from districts in which the initiative was supported by over 70 percent of district voters.[10] Efforts to change the law were aimed at making it applicable only to statewide offices other than state legislative offices. Presumably, because public funding provisions would make additional monies available to challengers, the law threatened the electoral safety of incumbent legislators. A month later, in a further act of resistance, the Massachusetts State Democratic Party turned off the microphones just as a resolution was about to be offered supporting the state's Clean Elections Law.[11]

The behavior of Democrats in the Massachusetts State Assembly raises some interesting questions about how policymakers perceive the effects of reform: Why would Democrats, who arguably benefit from public financing provisions, be so resistant to campaign finance reform? And why would incumbent politicians, not generally perceived as engaging in a great deal of altruistic behavior, resist legislation that would presumably make them safer (at least if one believes the arguments of campaign finance reform's opponents)? Are they all stalwart defenders of the First Amendment, believing that spending is somehow equated with free speech? Or is it as the *Boston Globe* editorial suggests, that changing from privately to publicly funded elections might put their seat at risk?

Opponents to reform would, of course, take issue with the idea that campaign reform puts incumbents at risk. Aside from the rhetoric, however, what do we really know about the consequences of reform? The answer is not nearly as much as the experts and participants often claim. First, analysis of new reform proposals is often based on what has happened in the past. The well-worn maxim that "those who fail to learn the lessons of history are doomed to repeat it" undoubtedly applies in this context, but there is considerable disagreement as to what the past can teach us about campaign reform. For opponents, the first and most important lesson of past reforms is that reform will always fail because of the stakes involved. Smart lawyers, cunning politicians, and devious consultants will find loopholes in even the most well-thought-out laws. Of course, smart lawyers also find ways out of criminal convictions, but rarely do we blame the law itself for individual criminal conduct, or for a lawyer's ability to save his client from criminal prosecution.

The second lesson of reform is that reform will have unintended consequences, many of which will be worse than the original problem. (If nothing else, strategic actors will attempt to manipulate the law to their advantage: lesson number one.) The classic example of unintended consequences is the growth of political action committees at the federal level as a result of campaign finance reforms in the 1970s. Often described as a sinister electoral force, PACs came into existence when labor unions, particularly the AFL-CIO, sought legal recognition of the groups they formed to raise and contribute money to candidates supporting their interests. The unintended result of the legal change was an exponential growth in the number of PACs, particularly those associated with business organizations. Ironically, many contemporary reform proposals at the federal level call for undoing this unintended consequence of the reform efforts of the 1970s.

For supporters of reform, the lessons to be drawn are much different. First, supporters contend reform does not work if it is not enforced. The Federal Election Commission (FEC), which has responsibility for regulating campaign finance behavior, has been described, among other things, as a "toothless watchdog."[12] Split evenly in terms of its partisan makeup and with its funding dependent on congressional approval, the FEC has lacked both the will and resources to enforce federal election laws. The combination of lax enforcement and relatively minor penalties for violations has encouraged candidates and parties to push the boundaries of federal election law, subsequently expanding the definition of legal activity with each new election cycle. Second, speaking directly to their critics, reformers have noted that though unintended consequences are likely, they hardly nullify the need for reform. In fact, taken to its logical conclusion, the law of unintended consequences is an argument for the status quo against any significant policy change, including reform in the areas of welfare and taxes.

Academic studies have generally been interpreted as more supportive of arguments against reform, but there is good reason to question the implications (if not the results) of this research. First, many of the conclusions regarding the implications of reform have been derived from studies done at the national level. While such studies undoubtedly provide insight into the failures of the Federal Election Campaign Act, the ability to draw conclusions about how modifications of campaign finance laws might affect electoral competition or voter turnout is necessarily limited. Studies at the state level, which have tended to focus on state legislative elections, have been much more mixed in their assessments of reform. Minnesota is generally provided as an example of where reform has worked. In Minnesota, public subsidies to legislative candidates have been sufficient to encourage compliance and electoral competition, though the effects on competition have been considerably less than reformers might have hoped.[13] Wisconsin, on the other hand, is generally offered as a model of an unsuccessful reform effort, where the public financing provisions were too low to entice compliance.[14] Competition declined as well, though it is unclear how much competition would have declined even without reform.

A final complicating factor emerges when discussing state reform efforts, and that is transferability. Minnesota's system may be relatively successful, but would it work in Indiana? Or Oregon? Or Connecticut? Moreover, as we saw in the case of Kentucky (see Introduction), reform efforts may appear to be successful in one electoral context but unsuccessful in another. Reform might enhance competition in gubernatorial elections even though it detracts from competition in legislative elections. Before we can further consider the effects of reform, we need to first outline the different components of reform (public disclosure, contribution limits, spending limits, and public financing) and their likely effects on the electoral process.

## PUBLIC DISCLOSURE

Public disclosure of campaign contributions and expenditures, the least intrusive and least controversial of reform efforts, is generally aimed at increasing political accountability. At least theoretically, full and open reporting of campaign fundraising activities allows voters to punish politicians for an overreliance on special interest contributions or for a reliance on contributions from the "wrong" type of interest group. For public disclosure to succeed as a mechanism of political accountability, however, several conditions must be met. First, candidates must accurately report on their campaign fundraising. Second, candidate fundraising data must be made available to voters *prior* to the actual election. And third, voters must be informed enough about candidate fundraising to at least potentially use that information in casting their ballot.

Although all three conditions are problematic, the third is the most questionable because it is unlikely voters would inform themselves of candidate fundraising efforts. In many elections, voters cannot identify either the name or the party of the candidates running for office.[15] The idea that voters would check campaign finance records to see which candidates received money from which of the thousands of PACs currently active in electoral politics is absurd. It is even more absurd to expect voters to examine individual contribution records. A more plausible but equally problematic scenario is that voters would learn about candidate fundraising after irregularities are publicized by strategic elites— opposition candidates, public interest groups, or the media. Voters could then punish those candidates engaging in questionable or unethical fundraising practices by not voting for them. There is some evidence that voters prefer reform-minded candidates. But in order for voters to identify these candidates, campaigns must provide full, accurate, and timely information about their fundraising activities. If campaigns delay reporting until after an election or if they intentionally obscure the sources of their fundraising, public disclosure fails as a means of increasing political accountability.

The 1996 presidential election in which Bill Clinton and the Democratic Party were accused of accepting illegal foreign contributions and mixing hard money accounts with soft money accounts illustrates several points. First, though serious questions were raised about Clinton fundraising efforts during the election, substantial evidence of misconduct surfaced only after the campaign was over. As a result, the allegations had little impact on the outcome of the election. Second, most voters largely disregarded the charges because they viewed both parties as equally corrupt. President Clinton selling access to the Lincoln Bedroom may have been a difference in degree but hardly seemed to be a difference in kind from former Speaker Newt Gingrich providing large contributors special access to Republican Congressional leadership in return for large soft money contributions. If money corrupts, there is little reason to believe that it corrupts Democrats more than Republicans, or that money from the Chinese government is more corrupting, or necessarily more adverse to the public interest, than money from Phillip Morris.

Accepting money from special interests has become such an institutionalized part of the political process that it is odd only when candidates do not accept such money. When it comes to the process by which competitive candidates raise money, there usually is not a dime's worth of difference between them. Consider, for example, John McCain's bid for the Republican nomination in the 2000 presidential election. McCain was criticized by the Bush campaign for supporting reform while accepting contributions and campaign support from special interests. Painting the opponent as a hypocrite may work well in electoral politics, but the Bush campaign knew very well that only the very wealthy can survive without special-interest contributions. In contemporary American politics, these are, with a few rare exceptions, the options: lose, spend your own money, or accept contributions from special interests. More to the point, public disclosure legitimizes these contributions so that voters are just as inclined to chastise candidates who appear to hypocritically accept contributions while claiming the mantle of reform as they are to reject candidates who enthusiastically raise as much money as humanly possible.

Despite the weaknesses of public disclosure, all fifty states require public disclosure of campaign fundraising practices for statewide elections. Despite being widely adopted, there is little evidence that public disclosure improves the electoral process. Elections are no more competitive nor are voters more trusting or more engaged in the political process. If anything, as voters have learned more about the fundraising activities of politicos, they have become less engaged and less trusting, and elections have become even less competitive. Overall, the advantages of public disclosure accrue primarily to the media who cover campaigns, the political professionals who can use published reports to identify future campaign contributors, and the academics who study campaign finance practices. Voters are neither better informed nor more engaged.[16]

Though it may be argued that public disclosure has succeeded in reducing overt corruption, it has also legitimated contributions from special interests. As Larry Sabato and Glenn Simpson observe:

> True enough, the cash bribe has become nearly extinct. And after Watergate some reasonably effective reforms were enacted that helped to correct specific ills observed in the Nixon scandals. Our politics *are* cleaner in some respects than they used to be. Yet time and again we have encountered disturbing practices that, upon reflection, can only be labeled corrupt and that cry out for change. . . . Indeed, influence peddling and other corruptions are in some ways more worrisome than they ever have been, because they are now so institutionalized that everyone practices them. The rules of the game, at least as perceived by the players, seem to demand it.[17]

While it is hard to argue against the merits of disclosure (and we are certainly not attempting to make that case here), arguments that public disclosure somehow improves the electoral process by enhancing accountability, or that greater public disclosure is all that is needed to cure what ails electoral politics, are, at best, overblown.

## CONTRIBUTION LIMITS

Three central rationales exist for contribution limits. They: (1) reduce corruption—or at least public perception of corruption—resulting from large contributions; (2) make the fundraising process more democratic by forcing candidates to raise money from a broader base of political supporters; and (3) reduce the overall level of candidate campaign spending by making the fundraising process more burdensome. Because of the *Buckley* decision limiting the ability of states to impose spending limits, many states have focused reform efforts on limiting campaign contributions. And though states vary widely in terms of their willingness to limit contributions from various sources, other than public disclosure requirements, contribution limits are the most widely adopted reform across the states.

## Contributions and Corruption

The principal logic of contribution limits centers around the idea of reducing the nexus between contributors and public officials. Even when there is no quid pro quo, even if no special access resulted, large contributions raise concerns about the appearance (if not the reality) of impropriety. Why, after all, would anyone give a million dollars to a candidate or a party if they did not expect something in return? Such altruism, particularly when it involves furthering someone else's political career, seems to defy common sense. Yet, benevolence is what opponents to campaign finance reform—as well as many academics— would have us believe. Contributors contribute but receive little more than returned phone calls, a few moments of time, or the satisfaction of knowing that they have helped candidates they believe in.

This position is not without support in the academic literature. Most studies examining the impact of roll call voting on legislative decision-making have either failed to find a significant impact of contributions on votes; or have found a marginal impact—limiting the connection to less visible and less salient votes.[18] Such findings, however, should be treated with a healthy dose of cynicism. Statistical evidence may indicate that campaign contributions do not *systematically* alter the voting decisions of legislators, but accepting the null hypothesis of statistically significant influence is not the same as saying that legislators—voting primarily on the basis of party, ideology, and constituency—are free of the influence of campaign contributions. Consider, for example, that you have just discovered that you have cancer. Your doctor informs you that with chemotherapy your chances for surviving are very good. In fact, in 95 percent of the cases, the cancer goes into remission and the patient lives a healthy, normal life. While the statistical evidence may reassure you a great deal, you have no real way of knowing whether you will be among the 95 percent that survive or among the 5 percent that do not. Nor does the 95 percent survival rate offer much reassurance if you are among the unlucky five.

Along these lines, opponents to reform are quick to note that most of the evidence of corruption is anecdotal—focusing on a single issue or a single legislator—and that more systematic studies fail to turn up evidence of a distorting influence of contributions on the legislative process. But the systematic evidence does not invalidate anecdotal evidence any more than a low crime rate invalidates a single murder.[19] Anecdotal evidence may be indicative of something outside of the ordinary, but that does not make it any less real or any less compelling. After all, how many savings and loan scandals does it take before the relationship between contributions and influence becomes statistically significant?

The Supreme Court itself recognized this distinction in its *Buckley v. Valeo* decision:

> Of almost equal concern as the danger of actual quid pro quo arrangements is the impact of the appearance of corruption stemming from public awareness of the opportunities for abuse inherent in a regime of large individual financial contributions.[20]

For the Court, anecdotal rather than statistical evidence was sufficient justification for contribution (though not for spending) limits.

Because legislators make hosts of decisions that are not recorded as roll call votes, the influence of contributions may be subtle and more difficult to detect. For example, the influence may show up in how a legislator changes language in mark-up sessions, where a single phrase can save industry billions of dollars. As former Senator William Proxmire observed:

> It may not come in a vote. It may come in a speech not delivered. The PAC payoff may come in a colleague not influenced. It may come in a calling off of a meeting that otherwise would result in advancing legislation. It may come in a minor change in one paragraph in a 240-page bill. It may come in a witness, not invited to testify before a committee.[21]

Campaign contributions are only the beginning of most efforts at influencing legislation. Contributions buy access, which in turn provides an opportunity for lobbyists to persuade legislators.[22] In this sense, the influence of campaign contributions may be less direct than is commonly assumed; but this is hardly the same as saying campaign contributions have no effect. Even if—as the conventional wisdom holds—information rather than money is the number one resource of the professional lobbyist,[23] money is critical in the dissemination of this information. As one recent study concludes: "By mastering the communications process and focusing on persuasive narratives, moneyed interests have carved out considerable power for themselves by their ability to define problems and acceptable solutions, as well as to lobby key policymakers."[24] And while moneyed interests have always exerted power, in contemporary American politics the only countervailing force to powerful moneyed interests are other competing, moneyed interests. Social movements, political parties, voters, even elected representatives no longer serve to challenge the dominance of powerful interest groups over the policymaking process. As Darrell West and Burdett Loomis conclude:

> Thirty years ago, social movements and investigative journalists were powerful forces. From the civil rights coalition to the consumer safety movement, there were demonstrated cases in which broadly defined societal interests demonstrated their ability to alter public policy. Today, the dominant forces are large,

usually corporate interests. The power to convey convincing narratives requires money and favors those who already are well-organized politically. Such an emphasis on moneyed interests weakens American democracy and threatens the very foundations of representative democracy.[25]

But even if money exerts an undeniable (though often subtle) influence on policy and policymakers, the question of whether contribution limits can reduce actual corruption—or at least public perceptions of corruption—remains subject to dispute. Contribution limits in federal elections, adopted in the early 1970s, have coincided with a steady decline in public trust, undoubtedly because federal contribution limits are easily and regularly skirted by candidates. Has the law failed to reduce perceptions of corruption? Or has the failure of the law added to public distrust? To date, there are no studies connecting relatively restrictive contribution limits with increased public confidence in state (or national) governments.

The Supreme Court has, however, reaffirmed its commitment to contribution limits based on the logic that large contributions provide the appearance of corruption. Writing for the majority in *Nixon v. Shrink Missouri Government PAC,* Justice David H. Souter discounted the weight of academic studies relative to anecdotal evidence and newspaper accounts, at least in part because academic studies offer contradictory assessments regarding the potentially corrupting influence of campaign contributions. As Justice Souter observed, "Given the conflict among these publications [academic studies], and the absence of any reason to think that public perception has been influenced by the studies cited by the respondents, there is little reason to doubt that sometimes large contributions will work actual corruption to our political system, and no reason to question the existence of a corresponding suspicion among voters."[26]

At this point, perhaps the best we can conclude is that large contributions continue to raise the specter of corruption, and that the specter alone is, at least according to current Supreme Court interpretation, sufficient to justify state regulation of campaign contributions. Having said that, however, there is little evidence at either the state or national level suggesting that limiting contributions affects either corruption or perceptions of corruption. In fact, unless other measures are taken to reduce the spending side of the campaign finance equation, public cynicism is likely to grow rather than recede as candidates devote increased time and energy to campaign fundraising, and as voters recognize the impotence of the law in controlling the power of moneyed interests.

## Contributions and Competition

The small individual contributor is as sacred in the American polity as the small business owner is in the American economy. Campaigns run on the basis of small contributions from middle-class Americans embody the democratic ideal of grassroots, participatory democracy. They are the Davids in American politics out to slay the proverbial Goliaths: candidates bought and paid for by wealthy contributors and corporate PACs. By limiting contributions, reformers hoped to reduce the power of wealthy patrons or "fat cats" who took it upon themselves to bankroll individual candidacies, usually in return for favorable public policies. Placing limits on the size of contributions would, ideally, force candidates to seek out a larger pool of small contributors. Removing, or at least limiting, the role of fat cats by reducing the size of individual contributions would, in turn, reap electoral benefits in terms of electoral competition by leveling the campaign fundraising playing field.

As reformers hoped, the actual number of citizens making campaign contributions has, in fact, increased since the 1960s—even as other forms of participation, most notably voter turnout, have declined.[27] Yet, campaign contributors, including those making smaller contributions, hardly resemble the average citizen: Notably, they are wealthier, better educated, more likely to be male and white, and conservative on economic issues.[28] Changes in campaign finance regulations have done little to alter this fundamental bias in American politics.[29] But forcing candidates to rely on smaller contributions does not means that candidates have stopped going where the money is. While campaigns have expanded their efforts so they are successfully raising money from a larger number of contributors, giving money remains a form of electoral participation dominated by the upper and middle classes. In other words, the democratization of campaign contributions may expand the base of elite contributors, but campaign fundraising is itself hardly a democratic enterprise. Even with current limits, a relatively small percentage of citizens can afford to give $1,000 to a candidate, and even among those who can afford to contribute, only a small percentage actually do so, and many in amounts of $25 or less. According to the Center for Responsive Politics, less than one-tenth of one percent of U.S. citizens contributed $1,000 or more in 1996, while approximately 80 percent of the citizenry contributed nothing at all. As such, raising or lowering limits is unlikely to drastically alter the total number of contributors. As evidence to this point, consider figure 2.1, which presents the percentage of respondents from the National Election Studies reporting that they contributed to a candidate between 1952 and 1996.

As the graph makes clear, the percentage of citizens contributing to a campaign has not increased over time despite the enactment of contribution limits. Nor has the adoption of limits at the federal level corresponded with an increase in electoral competition.[30] In addition, while campaigns that rely on small contributions are often more populist in tone, they are not always widely embraced. Oliver North's 1994 Senate campaign spent over $20 million, most of which was

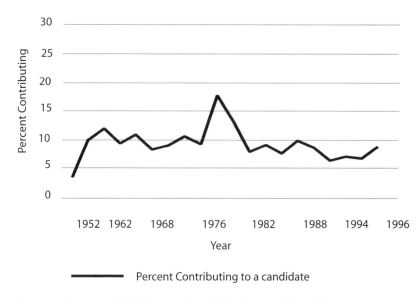

**Figure 2.1** Percentage of NES Respondents Who Reported Contributing to a Campaign, 1952–96

raised in small contributions.[31] North's reliance on small contributions neither limited his total spending nor assured his victory.

The more damning criticism of contribution limits is that lower limits increase the time and energy devoted to campaign fundraising activities. Common sense tells us that, all else being equal, it would take less time to raise $1 million from a hundred contributors than from a thousand contributors. But all else is rarely equal, and the same individual who has trouble generating $1,000 contributions is likely to have trouble generating $10,000 contributions. In fact, assuming that contributors are strategic rather than altruistic, there is reason to believe that allowing large contributions would inhibit rather than enhance nonincumbent fundraising efforts.

Many potential challengers, it is argued, opt out of an election because of the time and energy required to raise enough money just to be competitive. But how might increased contribution limits affect this particular decision-making calculus? The conventional wisdom is that increasing contribution limits would spur electoral competition by reducing the fundraising burden on nonincumbents. However, this logic assumes a relatively static definition of what it takes to be competitive. It also assumes that incumbents would be either unaffected by the policy change, or that the change would result in a reshuffling of the representative's priorities. That is, finding fundraising easier, incumbents would turn their attention to policymaking activities. This scenario is true, however, only if incumbents raise money strategically—responding primarily to some assessment of electoral need. If incumbents raise money to deter potential challengers,[32] higher contribution limits would serve as an incentive to raise more rather than less money.

Future elections pose considerable uncertainty about electoral conditions, the types of challenger, and issues that might emerge. This uncertainty serves as an impetus to raise more money than is necessary. Though higher contribution limits might help challengers raise more money in an absolute sense, there is reason to believe that the gap between rich and poor candidates would continue to expand as the rich got richer.

## PUBLIC FUNDING AND SPENDING LIMITS

Because of the *Buckley* decision, the question of candidate-based public funding is inevitably intertwined with spending limits. Several states provide public funding through the political parties without any associated limits. If the goal is maximizing electoral competition, parties are considered to be the most rational of contributors because they are more inclined to give to nonincumbent candidates than either individuals or political action committees. In this respect, party-based public funding mechanisms are thought to increase electoral competition by increasing the financial activity of state political parties. Party-based public funding is generally devoted to party maintenance activities and organizational overhead. Thus, the funding provides stability to party finances while freeing up other funds for electoral activity.[33] In terms of electoral impact, party-based public funding mechanisms are also thought to be particularly beneficial to the out-party or the minority party.[34] Given the diffuse nature of the support, however, it is unclear whether party-based public funding has a direct measurable effect in gubernatorial or legislative elections. Because the acceptance of public monies is not tied to any restriction on the parties' electoral activities, and because any potential effect is diffuse rather than candidate or party specific, it generally registers little or no public opposition. As a measure of reform, it also enjoys a healthy level of support among political scientists who generally prefer stronger, more responsible political parties.[35]

In direct contrast, candidate-based public funding mechanisms are almost always used as a lure to hook candidates on a set of corresponding spending limits. As a result, candidate-based public funding mechanisms are almost always mired in political and legal controversy. Though the mechanisms are often derided as welfare for politicians, most of the controversy surrounding them centers less on the public financing provisions than on the accompanying spending limits. For opponents to reform, spending limits not only violate the First Amendment, they also serve to reduce electoral competition and voter participation.

## Spending Limits and the First Amendment

In *Buckley v. Valeo* (1976), the Supreme Court struck down involuntary spending limits on the grounds that such limits violated First Amendment guarantees of free political expression. At the same time, however, the Court allowed contribution limits to stand, arguing that such limits must be balanced against the need to protect the integrity of democratic processes. Because the connection between campaign spending and perceptions of corruption was much thinner, spending limits were considered unconstitutional. The Court did, however, allow "voluntary" spending limits; that is, limits predicated on the acceptance of public funding. In the Court's opinion, speech could be subsidized but not limited, or perhaps more accurately, speech could be limited only if it was first subsidized.

Since the *Buckley* decision, the politics of campaign finance reform have been irrevocably linked to the First Amendment as opponents have cloaked arguments against reform in the language of the *Buckley* decision, often proclaiming that "money is speech." Though the Supreme Court certainly came close, it never quite equated money with speech, instead noting that the connection between campaign spending and speech is so close that reducing campaign spending in the political process was the equivalent of reducing the amount of gasoline in a car. Money fueled speech, but it was not speech itself.[36] Moreover, in defending the spending limits, the state argued that spending limits were necessary to maintain some semblance of political equality; the Court rejected the idea that either perceptions of corruption or political equality presented a compelling justification to enforce mandatory limits on candidate spending.

In rulings since *Buckley,* the Court has maintained the distinction between contributions and expenditures. The decision itself, however, has come under increasing criticism from both sides of the reform debate. Supreme Court Justice Clarence Thomas, who has never met a contribution limit that he believed passed constitutional muster, noted repeatedly that he would like the *Buckley* precedent overturned. For Thomas, contributing unlimited sums to political candidates is a fundamental constitutional right. On the other side of the debate, New York Law Professor Burt Neuborne argues, "*Buckley* is hardly a model for the formulation of public policy. The per curiam opinion resulted in the distortion of Congress's intent, imposed a regime on the nation that no Congress would ever have enacted, and, most importantly, has created a campaign finance system abhorred by virtually all the participants."[37]

Though the Court's recent ruling in *Nixon v. Shrink Missouri Government PAC* dealt primarily with the question of contribution limits, in separate opinions Justices Kennedy, Thomas, Stevens, and Breyer all noted a willingness to reconsider *Buckley.* Whether this means the Court's decisions would be more or less supportive of reform is doubtful. As Neuborne observes, "The Court could push the tree upon reformers by eviscerating the distinction between contributions and expenditures and then deciding that neither may be constitutionally regulated."[38] The Supreme Court itself, Neuborne writes, appears to be divided into three camps. Justices Thomas, Rehnquist, Scalia, and Kennedy appear to support overturning limits on contributions, while Justices Stevens and Ginsburg appear willing to allow greater government regulation of both spending and contributions. Adding uncertainty to the mix, Justices O'Connor, Souter, and Breyer appear to be undecided. Regardless of the balance on the Court, the framework used to determine the constitutionality of campaign reform may be significantly altered over the course of the next several years.

But even if the framework were not altered, there is reason to believe that significant reform can emerge within the confines of the *Buckley* decision. Even as mandatory spending limits were declared unconstitutional, the presidential system of public funding, with its combination of public grants and spending limits, was upheld. This determination means spending limits are unconstitutional only when they are not connected to some form of public financing. As the Court observed, "Rather than abridging, restricting, or censoring speech, [public financing of presidential campaigns] represents an effort to use public money to facilitate and enlarge public discussion and participation in the electoral process."[39] The criterion, then, for determining constitutionality of a public financing scheme rests on whether the system is truly voluntary, or whether it is voluntary in name but coercive in effect.[40] Systems which offer generous inducements for compliance with spending limits might be considered coercive if they put a candidate not accepting the inducement at a significant disadvantage, Generally, however, systems that rely on inducements (public subsidies) to encourage compliance have been upheld, while systems that punish candidates for rejecting spending limits have been thrown out.[41] While almost any public financing scheme is going to be subjected to at least one court challenge, where states combine public financing provisions with reasonable spending limits, the laws are likely to pass constitutional muster.

### Spending Limits and Electoral Competition

Another objection to public funding rests on the claim that spending limit provisions (even with public financing) protect incumbents. The empirical evidence on this point, however, is far from conclusive. Consider, for example, that since the Federal Election Campaign Act was passed three incumbent presidents (Ford, Carter, and Bush) have been defeated while only two have won reelection (Reagan and Clinton). Moreover, Clinton's 1996 reelection effort all but obliterated existing campaign finance regulations.

At the state level, there is no evidence that gubernatorial incumbents are made more secure by either candidate- or party-based public financing provisions.[42] Because states have been less willing to supply public financing to state legislative candidates, the mixed experiences of Minnesota and Wisconsin candidate-based public financing in state legislative races serve as the main evidence. The general conclusion is that public funding of state legislative races has been more successful in Minnesota than in Wisconsin, largely because the public funding in Minnesota is sufficient to entice a broader level of compliance. Nevertheless, the most exhaustive study to date concludes that there is simply not enough evidence to reach a verdict on the question of public financing.[43]

Undeterred by the inconclusive evidence, reformers and opponents both continue making claims about the electoral consequences of candidate-based public funding, though it is opponents who most often lay claim to the mantle of empirical "truth." This truth, however, is based not on the evidence from the states or from presidential elections, but on observed correlations between campaign spending and electoral outcomes in congressional elections. (Ironically, as one of the repercussions of the *Buckley* decision, congressional elections are conducted without public financing or spending limits.) At first glance, these correlations seem to tell us that challengers yield a bigger electoral bang for their campaign dollars and that incumbents receive little or no return on their campaign spending.[44] If this were truly the case, it would be easy to see why spending limits would hurt challengers, while having little or no effect on incumbents. Challengers need to spend money in order to be competitive. Limiting challenger spending would, subsequently, have negative consequences on the challenger's share of the vote. Further, the more draconian the limits, the greater the damage. Yet, this finding has been subjected to repeated challenges within the academic literature, most notably by Donald Green and Jonathan Krasno who find "salvation for spendthrift incumbents." They contend that while the effect of incumbent spending may be smaller than the effect of challenger spending, it is significant. Because incumbents typically raise (and spend) more money than challengers, the yield on incumbent spending is considerably greater than the yield on challenger spending.[45]

Still, opponents to reform have successfully labeled legislative efforts to reform the federal system of campaign finance as "incumbency protection acts." Not only does the label ignore more recent research on the relationship between spending and votes but it also ignores the public financing side of the equation. In congressional elections, the majority of challengers spend less than any proposed limit (even if the limit were placed at $600,000). In theory, public financing provisions should result in an across-the-board increase in challenger spending, and subsequently, an across-the-board increase in the average challenger share of the vote. However, it is possible that a combination of public financing and spending limits could hurt the chances of well-funded challengers in competitive races against vulnerable incumbents, a threat that is probably overstated by opponents of reform. First, most congressional incumbents who are defeated are guilty of an ethical impropriety, have become vulnerable because of their voting record, or are simply from a highly competitive district—not because they have been outspent. While opponents to reform often hold the outdated belief that incumbent spending does not matter, it is at least arguable that were these endangered incumbents to spend less, they would become even more vulnerable. Second, though opponents to reform are quick to note that money does not buy elections in other contexts (e.g., "electoral bang" and "yield," both referring to votes or rather the return on spending in vote percentages), they seem to believe that its purchasing power is virtually unlimited for nonincumbents.

Two general principles apply here. First, campaign spending is subject to the law of diminishing returns, meaning that after candidates reach a certain threshold, each additional dollar buys less in terms of the final percentage of the vote. Second, money is necessary but not sufficient to win an election. Candidates need enough money to establish name recognition and to get their message out, but assuming the message reaches a wide enough audience, the message rather than the money wins the election. For candidates who currently find it difficult to raise money, public financing provisions help them to at least get out their message, a feat that is often impossible in a system based entirely on private contributions. A privately funded campaign finance system may exert heavy pressure on first-time candidates who often enter electoral politics without a fundraising organization already in place. The more expensive campaigning becomes, the heavier the pressure becomes as the candidates must worry about having enough money to deliver their messages. As a result, many potential candidates may opt out of the electoral process because they lack relevant fundraising experience. But even experienced candidates (state legislators, city council members, school board members, etc.) may opt out of a race if they have concerns about the amount of time and energy required to raise enough money just to be competitive. Public financing provisions can enhance electoral competition by encouraging candidates to run, particularly politically experienced candidates who might otherwise have opted out of the race.

The overall electoral effect of a combination of candidate-based public financing and spending limits likely depends on the level of public funding and the level of any associated spending limits. Available evidence simply does not support broad generalizations that spending limits diminish (or enhance) electoral competition. Public funding must be high enough to entice compliance, to induce candidates to enter the race, and to jumpstart other fundraising efforts; but not so high as to call into question the voluntary nature of the limits. Spending limits must also be high enough to assure that nonincumbents can run competitive races, otherwise incumbents, already a protected species, might be even further removed from any sign of electoral vulnerability. Yet, if spending limits become too high, they become meaningless in terms of their effect on candidate spending.

## Spending Limits and Political Participation

A related objection to spending limits is that they have a negative effect on voter participation, most notably voter turnout. Where states adopt spending limits provisions, the reasoning goes, campaigns will devote less money to voter registration and voter turnout drives, instead devoting their limited resources to television advertising. As a corollary, competitive campaigns attract voters, and competitive campaigns are generally more expensive than uncompetitive ones. If reduced spending negatively affects electoral competition, it should have subsequent effects on voter participation.

Although the connection between campaign spending and voter turnout appears unassailable, in practice, things are rarely so simple. First, in studies that have examined the relationship between campaign spending and voter turnout, there is often a statistically significant relationship, but the actual effect of campaign spending on voter turnout is generally quite small, meaning that substantial changes in spending would have only a limited effect on the number of voters turning out on election day, or on the probability that any particular individual voted. Second, there is something of a paradox in the literature. Over the last several decades, campaign spending has increased dramatically, even after accounting for inflation, but voter turnout has steadily declined. If campaign spending really increased voter turnout, we should be experiencing an increase, rather than a drop, in voter turnout. Finally, one of the central arguments for campaign reform is that it deals with perceptions of corruption. If voters believe the electoral process is more fair and less corrupt, reform may have indirect effects on voter participation. As with electoral competition, the evidence is much more mixed, and much less conclusive, than either reformers or opponents would have us believe.

## CONCLUSIONS

We began this chapter by noting that though reform is often discussed as an aggregate, it is, in reality, a collection of measures each with a different purpose and set of intended and actual consequences. These various measures could potentially be combined into unlimited "comprehensive" reform packages, suggesting there could be unlimited sets of potential effects, some positive, some negative. In this respect, the rhetoric of reform is based on an overly simplified question: Does reform enhance or diminish democratic governance? To truly understand the consequences of reform, however, one must ask a fundamentally different question: Which types of reform have which types of effects on the electoral process? We might also add a further consideration: What are the effects of various types of reform across varying electoral contexts? Though there is a multitude of potential effects, in this book our primary focus will be on the effects of reform on campaign spending, electoral competition, and voter turnout.

# CHAPTER 3

# Patterns of Spending in Gubernatorial Elections

American elections are expensive and getting more expensive every electoral cycle. This growth in campaign spending has been well documented for presidential, U.S. Senate, U.S. congressional elections, and state legislative elections.[1] At the national level, the rate of increase in campaign spending has far exceeded the inflation rate.[2] Many Americans now believe that if you want to run for a major elective office in the United States, you need to be either personally wealthy or have a large number of affluent friends. The "common man," the "little guy," is perceived as being shut out of the American electoral process.

It is these feelings, these views, which help fuel the call for campaign finance reform. Americans are uncomfortable with a system that apparently uses wealth, or wealthy friends, as a criterion for public office. Perhaps if we could just hold down the costs of running for office, they think, we could reacquire the American dream where anyone can grow up to be president, a senator, or a congressperson. Of course, the American dream of anybody being able to grow up to become president has always been more myth than reality. Wealth has always given one an advantage when running for office in America, and lacking wealth or wealthy friends has always been an impediment when seeking office. Despite reform efforts at the national level, the dream remains unfeasible for most Americans as campaign costs continue to rise. Nevertheless, the high cost of running for a major elective office in America is likely to remain at the center of discussions on campaign finance and campaign finance reform.

In this chapter, we examine the basic parameters of spending in gubernatorial elections. We begin by examining the growth in spending in gubernatorial elections over the last twenty years. We compare this pattern of growth with that of U.S. senate and U.S. congressional elections. Next we look at which states tend to have very expensive gubernatorial elections and which states tend to have less expensive races. We discuss how population size, geographic size, and economic well-being condition the cost of elections. We conclude by again considering the relationships among spending in gubernatorial, U.S. senate, and U.S. house elections.

## GUBERNATORIAL SPENDING: 1978 TO 1998

In 1978, the most expensive gubernatorial contest was in New York, where approximately $12 million was spent.[3] Just twenty years later, the California gubernatorial race became the nation's most expensive in history when over $120 million was spent by all of the candidates over the primary and general election cycles.[4] This precedent-setting 1998 California election was 1000 percent higher than the most expensive race in 1978. Over the period of 1978 to 1998, thirteen states had gubernatorial elections which were over 500 percent more expensive than the state's earliest gubernatorial election in the period.[5] In 1998, fifteen of the thirty-six states that had gubernatorial elections set spending records during their combined primary and general electoral period.

Gubernatorial campaign spending in the United States increased more than 478 percent over the twenty-year period. In the thirty-six states that had gubernatorial elections in 1998, over $469 million was spent by all of the candidates who ran for governor. The mean, or average, spent in each state was approximately $13,030,000. In the thirty-six states that had gubernatorial elections in 1978, by contrast, only a little over $98 million was spent by all of the candidates, a mean of approximately $2,732,000 per state.[6] Gubernatorial elections have become very expensive affairs indeed.

Of course, the cost of running for governor differs among the states and across the time period. While the California governor's race cost over $120 million in 1998, the total cost of the 1998 governor's race in Wyoming was less than $800,000. The California governor's race cost "only" about $8.5 million in 1978, which was the same year that candidates in Vermont spent a little over $110,000 to run for governor. But one needs to be very careful when making monetary comparisons of the states' gubernatorial elections.[7]

Table 3.1 gives the four-year running means, or running averages, of statewide costs for all gubernatorial elections from 1978 to 1998.[8] So, for example, the entry for 1981 provides the mean cost per state for all gubernatorial elections from 1978 to 1981 while the entry for 1998 provides the mean cost per state for all elections from 1995 to 1998.[9] The table presents totals for actual dollar amounts spent by all candidates in both the primary and general elections, as well as totals of the mean cost per state for all candidates in both the primary

**Table 3.1** Four-Year Average Total State Campaign Costs in Gubernatorial Elections, 1978–98

| Years | Total Primary and General Election Spending | | Democratic and Republican Nominees |
|---|---|---|---|
| | All Candidates | | |
| | Real Dollars | Constant 1992 Dollars | Constant 1992 Dollars |
| 1978–81 | 3,543,912 | 6,460,400 | 5,095,871 |
| 1979–82 | 5,080,006 | 7,633,367 | 5,747,700 |
| 1980–83 | 5,213,748 | 7,577,149 | 5,840,140 |
| 1981–84 | 5,427,327 | 7,633,719 | 5,597,867 |
| 1982–85 | 5,320,112 | 7,387,368 | 5,678,921 |
| 1986 | 6,969,689 | 8,815,996 | 6,275,622 |
| 1987 | 6,857,872 | 8,408,233 | 5,937,776 |
| 1988 | 7,086,005 | 8,538,503 | 6,357,749 |
| 1989 | 7,644,539 | 9,092,438 | 6,669,525 |
| 1990 | 9,090,215 | 9,728,065 | 7,271,464 |
| 1991 | 9,061,017 | 9,784,420 | 7,347,388 |
| 1992 | 9,213,987 | 9,778,770 | 7,162,368 |
| 1993 | 8,988,779 | 9,432,951 | 6,951,078 |
| 1994 | 10,352,753 | 9,972,205 | 7,338,454 |
| 1995 | 10,373,129 | 9,927,671 | 7,244,461 |
| 1996 | 10,732,903 | 10,164,418 | 7,441,089 |
| 1997 | 10,903,223 | 10,263,421 | 7,658,881 |
| 1998 | 11,888,494 | 10,634,849 | 7,859,612 |

and general elections measured in constant 1992 dollars.[10] In addition, the table gives the mean cost per state of running in both the primary and general elections for only the Democratic Party and Republican Party nominees (measured in constant 1992 dollars).

As is evident from table 3.1, the average cost of running for governor steadily edged upward from 1981 to 1998. The mean cost in constant dollars rose over 250 percent from 1981 to 1998, while the mean actual dollar costs grew over 335 percent over the same period. Although inflation clearly impacted the cost of running for office, as both the real dollar and constant dollar figures show, the costs associated with running for governor still rose faster than the rate of inflation. Even when constant dollars are used to control for the effect of inflation, from 1981 to 1998, the average total cost per state for gubernatorial elections rose over 160 percent and the monies spent by the nominees of the two major parties rose over 150 percent.

After reviewing research on the rising cost of running for the U.S. Congress, it should come as no surprise that the cost of running for governor is also rising

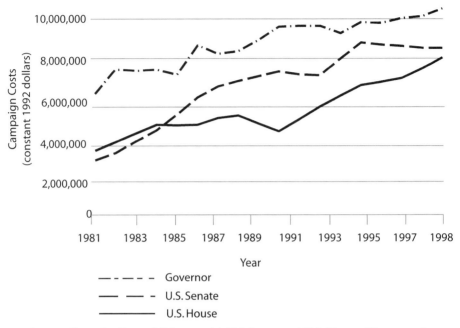

**Figure 3.1** Campaign Costs of Gubernatorial, U.S. Senate, and U.S. House of Representatives Elections, 1981–98

with no apparent end in sight. Figure 3.1 portrays the rising cost of running for governor, the U.S. Senate, and the U.S. House of Representatives. Each data point for the gubernatorial plot represents the total amount of money spent, in constant 1992 dollars, by all candidates in both the primary and general elections for the average state in a given four-year period. Each data point for the U.S. House plot represents the average level of expenditures spent, in constant 1992 dollars, by all candidates running for Congress in a state in a given four-year period.[11] Finally, each data point for the U.S. Senate plot represents the average level of expenditures spent, in constant 1992 dollars, by all candidates running for the Senate in a state in a given six-year period.[12]

A number of facts can be gleaned from examining figure 3.1. First, gubernatorial elections began the period of 1981 to 1998 being the most expensive of the three types of elections and remained the most expensive over the entire period. Second, while average statewide expenditures on U.S. House races were greater than those for U.S. Senate elections in the beginning of the time series, expenditures on U.S. Senate races began to exceed U.S. House races around 1985 and have continued to exceed them ever since. And third, the average cost for all three types of elections has continued to rise, well above the inflation rate, over the time period. Controlling for the effect of inflation, the average total statewide cost of campaigns has risen 268 percent, 222 percent, and 165 percent for U.S. Senate, U.S. House, and gubernatorial elections, respectively.

One way to judge how the trend towards more expensive campaigns in one type of election is related to the trend towards more expensive campaigns in another type of election is to examine the correlations among the three trend lines shown in figure 3.1. A correlation of 1.0 between any two of the series would indicate that they co-vary, or go together, perfectly. A correlation of 0.0 would indicate that there is no relationship between the growing cost for one type of election and that of another.[13] The correlation between the growth in cost for gubernatorial elections and that for U.S. Senate elections seen in figure 3.1 is .94, while it is .83 for the relationship between gubernatorial and U.S. House elections. The correlation between U.S. Senate and U.S. House elections is .91. The trends for all three types of elections co-vary very strongly.

A final way to evaluate the growth in statewide average total cost of these elections is to use regression to specify how much each type of election tends to increase each year. This can be accomplished by regressing a year/counter on the data used to create figure 3.1.[14] If the counter is measured in units of 1, 0 to 17, the unstandardized regression coefficient will indicate how much, on average, the cost of a given type of election increases with each passing year.

Using regression analysis with deflated total spending data results in unstandardized regression coefficients of 214,750; 335,533; and 226, 370 for gubernatorial, U.S. Senate, and U.S. House elections, respectively. While gubernatorial elections had the highest statewide average cost at the beginning and at the end of the time series, the average rate of growth for gubernatorial elections was the smallest of the three types of elections: growing at a rate of only $214,750 per year. The average statewide cost of U.S. House elections grew a bit faster than gubernatorial elections. U.S. Senate races, however, grew at the fastest rate: approximately $335,534 per year, or almost 50 percent more than gubernatorial elections. If these differential growth rates continue, U.S. Senate races should become more expensive than gubernatorial elections by 2005.

Thus, the data presented so far indicate that spending on gubernatorial and other major elections in the United States rose steadily from 1981 to 1998, outstripping the inflation rate. Though the cost of gubernatorial elections varied greatly, the rising average cost of gubernatorial elections co-varied strongly with that of U.S. Senate and U.S. House elections. And while the average cost of gubernatorial elections is much higher than that of the average statewide costs of U.S. Senate and U.S. House elections for the entire time series, the rate of growth in the total cost of gubernatorial elections is actually smaller than that of U.S. Senate and U.S. House elections.

Next we explore the reasons behind the differential costs of U.S. gubernatorial elections. We will briefly examine whether the states that tend to have more expensive gubernatorial elections also tend to have expensive U.S. Senate and U.S. House elections. We will also examine which states tend to have very expensive gubernatorial elections and which states tend to have less expensive ones. Finally, we will consider how a state's population size, geographic size, and economic well-being condition the cost of elections.

## YES, SIZE DOES MATTER

In the previous section of this chapter we showed that the rising average cost of gubernatorial elections tended to co-vary with the rising average cost of U.S. Senate and U.S. House elections. But it might be the case that, despite the co-variation in average spending over time, states that have more expensive gubernatorial elections are not necessarily the ones that have more expensive U.S. Senate and U.S. House elections.[15] Table 3.2 directly addresses this issue. Table 3.2 portrays the correlations among total spending in gubernatorial elections, senior senator elections, junior senator elections, and congressperson elections for the period of 1992 to 1998.[16]

As can be seen in table 3.2, while the correlations are far from unity, the total costs of these elections do tend to co-vary. With the exception of the correlation between total spending in junior senators' races and U.S. representatives' elections, which is slightly higher than the rest, all of the correlations are very similar to each other. All of the correlations are statistically significant at the .01 level. So, while the focus of this book is on gubernatorial elections, the levels of these correlations and their similarity strongly suggests that there are some fundamental factors which drive the costs of all of these elections. In this section, we examine the importance of population size, geographic size, and economic well-being as determinants of the costs of elections.

Table 3.3 shows, in constant 1992 dollars, the twenty most expensive and twenty least expensive gubernatorial elections from 1978 to 1998. What should be most evident from this list is that, with a few exceptions such as Louisiana in

**Table 3.2** Correlations among the Total Costs of Gubernatorial, U.S. Senior Senator, U.S. Junior Senator, and U.S. Representative Elections, 1992–98*

|  | Governor | Senior Senator | Junior Senator | U.S. Representative |
|---|---|---|---|---|
| Governor | 1.00 |  |  |  |
| Senior Senator | .72 | 1.00 |  |  |
| Junior Senator | .72 | .74 | 1.00 |  |
| U.S. Representative | .79 | .73 | .85 | 1.00 |

*All correlations are statistically significant at the .01 level.

**Table 3.3** The Twenty Most Expensive and Twenty Least Expensive Gubernatorial Elections, 1978–98*

| Rank | Most Expensive | Least Expensive |
|------|----------------|-----------------|
| 1 | California, 1998 | Vermont, 1996 |
| 2 | California, 1994 | Vermont, 1978 |
| 3 | California, 1990 | Vermont, 1994 |
| 4 | Texas, 1990 | South Dakota, 1982 |
| 5 | Texas, 1986 | Vermont, 1992 |
| 6 | Florida, 1986 | Vermont, 1980 |
| 7 | Louisiana, 1979 | Delaware, 1980 |
| 8 | New York, 1998 | Vermont, 1982 |
| 9 | Pennsylvania, 1994 | Rhode Island, 1982 |
| 10 | New York, 1982 | North Dakota, 1980 |
| 11 | California, 1982 | Montana, 1984 |
| 12 | Texas, 1982 | Wyoming, 1998 |
| 13 | Georgia, 1998 | Delaware, 1996 |
| 14 | New York, 1994 | Georgia, 1978 |
| 15 | New Jersey, 1981 | North Dakota, 1992 |
| 16 | New Jersey, 1989 | North Dakota, 1988 |
| 17 | California, 1986 | Vermont, 1990 |
| 18 | Florida, 1990 | New Hampshire, 1994 |
| 19 | Tennessee, 1994 | North Dakota, 1984 |
| 20 | Illinois, 1990 | Utah, 1996 |

*These rankings are determined on the basis of the total cost for all candidates in both the primary and general elections, measured in constant 1992 dollars.

1979, Georgia in 1998, and Tennessee in 1994, the most expensive gubernatorial elections tend to occur in the states with the largest populations. Fourteen of the twenty most expensive races occurred in the six most populous states.[17] Predictably, the least expensive races tend to occur in the least populated states. Fifteen of the twenty least expensive races occurred in the seven least populated states of the United States.[18] The information given in table 3.3 suggests that population size might be a critical factor in affecting the total cost of gubernatorial elections.

There are a number of good reasons to expect that a state's population size might critically affect the cost of its gubernatorial elections. First and foremost, political campaigns are about communicating to people. The more people there are to contact in a state, the greater the cost of campaigning. Political campaign costs began to significantly expand in the United States as the population of the electorate started expanding in the 1820s and 1830s.[19] Larger states tend to have more congressional elections with a greater statewide competition. Election from a larger state, such as California and New York, may be seen as "prestigious," either as a value unto itself or as a steppingstone to the presidency, thus serving as incentive for candidates to engage in a vigorous campaign.[20] The largest states also tend to have the largest and most expensive television markets in the United States. Much of the cost of contemporary campaigns is tied to the cost of television advertising. As such, more expensive television markets mean more expensive campaigns. Finally, the size of government may affect the cost of elections. As governments do more and expend more money, more stakeholders take an interest in what government does and expend their resources—money—to try and influence the outcomes of elections. Following this line of argument, since larger states tend to expend more tax dollars, one would likely see more stakeholders giving larger amounts of money trying to influence the outcomes of elections.

Population size is not the only size factor, however, that affects the cost of elections. Geographic size, as measured by the square mileage of a state, is an additional consideration when evaluating the costs of elections. If a candidate needs to contact a given number of people over a large area, not only will transportation costs be high but also media costs, as more television, radio, and newspaper outlets must be used. As such, it can be hypothesized that the larger the geographic size of a state, the greater the cost of elections, assuming all other factors are held constant.

The economic well-being of a state is another factor that may affect the cost of elections. As noted numerous times, statewide elections can be expensive affairs where candidates must depend upon contributions, personal wealth, or state monies to run a competitive race. The competition for contributions may also be a concern for candidates, since the pool of potential contributors and the pool of money that can potentially be contributed are not boundless. Very simply, there is only so much money that can be contributed.[21] The economic well-being, or wealth, of a state can affect the ability of contributors to contribute money. Further, the greater the amount of money that can be contributed will likely result in more money being contributed. It can be hypothesized, therefore, that the greater the economic well-being of a state, the greater the cost of elections, all other factors being held constant.

Table 3.4 seems to indicate that there is a strong relationship between the population size of a state and the total cost of a state's gubernatorial elections, a correlation of .75.[22] Similarly, there is a strong relationship between the cost of a state's gubernatorial elections and the total personal income in a state, a correlation of .82. It does not appear, however, that there is a strong relationship between geographic size and the cost of gubernatorial elections. The correlation is only .10 and it is not statistically significant.

Of course, an examination of simple correlations, by themselves, can be problematic when attempting to examine how a set of variables affects a given dependent variable. This is especially true when, as in the case of table 3.4, two

**Table 3.4** Correlations among Total Spending in Gubernatorial Elections, State Voting Age Population, Total State Personal Income, and State Geographic Size

| | Gubernatorial Election Costs | Voting Age Population | Personal Income | Geographic Size |
|---|---|---|---|---|
| **Gubernatorial Election Cost** | 1.00 | | | |
| **Voting Age Population** | .75* | 1.00 | | |
| **Personal Income** | .82* | .93* | 1.00 | |
| **Geographic Size** | .10 | .09 | .09 | 1.00 |

*Correlation is statistically significant at the .01 level; N = 302.

or more of the variables are themselves highly related. As shown in table 3.4, the total personal income in a state and the state's voting age population are highly related to each other, a correlation of .93. In fact, this is the highest correlation in table 3.4. The strong relationship between population and total personal income should not be considered surprising. States with larger populations ought to have a higher total income even if their per capita income rates are lower than those of states with relatively small populations. Given that a state's population is likely to drive both the total amount of spending in a state's gubernatorial election and its total personal income, it is important to control for the population size when attempting to evaluate the importance of income and state geographic size to spending in gubernatorial elections.

Equation 3.1 shows the results of a regression of total gubernatorial spending, in constant

$$(3.1) \quad Y = 1.71 + .195X_1 + 10.92X_2 + e \qquad \text{r squared} = .27$$

1992 dollars, per voting age citizen on personal income per voting age citizen and state geographic size where

$Y$ = spending in a state's gubernatorial elections (primary and general elections), in constant 1992 dollars, per voting age citizen;

$X_1$ = geographic size of the state measured in square mile units of 10,000; and

$X_2$ = personal income, in $1,000 units, per voting age citizen.

In order to evaluate this equation, it is important to understand certain parameters associated with the dependent variable. The mean value of total spending per voting age citizen in gubernatorial elections is 3.33, with a standard deviation of 3.33. The range of the dependent variable is from .22 in Georgia in 1986 to 31.5 in Alaska in 1986. So, the coefficient associated with the geographic size variable, statistically significant at the .01 level, indicates that for every additional 10,000 square miles in a state there is, on average, an additional 19.5 cents spent per voting age citizen in gubernatorial elections, all other variables being held constant.[23] Unlike the evidence suggested by the earlier correlational analysis, this regression analysis provides strong support for the proposition that the geographic size of a state is an important factor in conditioning the expected rate of spending in gubernatorial elections. This conclusion is in line with the arguments made in favor of the importance of geographic size.[24] Holding population size and personal income constant, the larger the geographic size of the state, the more it costs to run an election.

The coefficient in equation 3.1 associated with the personal income per voting age citizen variable, however, is not statistically significantly different from 0 (p = .53). Contrary to expectations, and the implication of the correlational analysis, per capita income does not seem to have an effect on spending in gubernatorial elections. The regression analysis shown in equation 3.1 suggests that the strong positive zero order correlation between total personal income and total spending in gubernatorial elections is primarily the result of the strong positive correlation between the voting age population of a state and the total personal income in a state.[25]

The implication of these results is that *size does matter* when evaluating the total cost of gubernatorial elections. Of particular significance is the voting age population of a state. Those states with large populations will tend to be the states with the most expensive gubernatorial elections. The importance of the population variable is such that it must be taken into account, or controlled for, when attempting to evaluate the importance of other variables relative to the cost of gubernatorial elections.

Once one takes into account the importance of population, the geographic size of a state affects the cost of gubernatorial elections. The cost per voting age citizen in gubernatorial elections tends to be larger, on average, the larger the geographic size of a state. It tends to cost more to contact 100,000 voters if they are spread out over 100,000 square miles than if they are spread out over 50,000 square miles.

The economic wealth of a state does seem to affect the total cost of gubernatorial elections but only because states that have larger populations also tend to have more total wealth. The strong positive correlation between total personal income and total spending in gubernatorial elections seems to result primarily from the effect of population. Once one controls for the effect of population size, the correlation between spending and personal income approaches zero; the correlation between spending in gubernatorial elections per voting age citizen and personal income per voting age citizen is .03 and not statistically significant. Personal income per voting age citizen does not have a statistically significant effect on the total cost per voting age citizen in gubernatorial elections when controlling for the effect of geographic size (equation 3.1).

## SIZE AND GUBERNATORIAL, U.S. SENATE, AND U.S. HOUSE ELECTIONS

Earlier in this chapter we established that the cost totals for gubernatorial elections behave in many ways like the cost totals for U.S. Senate and U.S. House elections. The average statewide costs for all three types of elections rose sharply over the period of 1978 to 1998, along trend lines that tended to co-vary to a significant degree. And the statewide costs for gubernatorial, U.S. Senate, and U.S. House elections also showed very strong positive correlations for the period of 1992 to 1998. Having established the importance of population size and geographic size as factors that help shape the cost of gubernatorial elections, we now use those factors in reconsidering the interrelationships of gubernatorial, U.S. Senate, and U.S. House elections.

The importance of population to the relationships among the costs of gubernatorial, U.S. Senate, and U.S. House elections can be seen by analyzing the correlations among these elections on the basis of cost per voting age citizen. These correlations are given in table 3.5. As should be readily apparent, these correlations are very different from those seen in table 3.2, which were highly positive and statistically significant. The only positive and statistically significant correlations in table 3.5 are those among the different types of congressional elections. All of the correlations between the cost of gubernatorial elections per voting age citizen and the cost of congressional elections per voting age citizen are slightly negative and none of them are statistically significant.[26] A comparison of the correlations in table 3.2 with those in table 3.5 strongly suggests that it is population that drives the apparently strong positive relationships that are often seen between the average total statewide costs of gubernatorial elections and the average total statewide costs of U.S. Senate and U.S. House elections. By contrast, relation-

**Table 3.5** Correlations among the Costs per Voting Age Citizen of Gubernatorial, U.S. Senior Senator, U.S. Junior Senator, and U.S. Representative Elections, 1992–98

|  | Governor | Senior Senator | Junior Senator | U.S. Representative |
|---|---|---|---|---|
| **Governor** | 1.00 | | | |
| **Senior Senator** | − .07 | 1.00 | | |
| **Junior Senator** | − .13 | .44* | 1.00 | |
| **U.S. Representative** | − .02 | .56* | .49* | 1.00 |

*Correlation is statistically significant at the .05 level.

ships between the average total statewide costs of senatorial elections and those of U.S. House elections remain even when they are specified on the basis of cost per voting age citizen. It appears, on a cost per voting age citizen basis, that gubernatorial elections are indeed very different from U.S. Senate and U.S. House elections.

Earlier, in the discussion of equation 3.1, it was shown that a state's geographic size, not its personal income per voting age citizen, had a statistically significant effect on the cost of gubernatorial elections. Table 3.6 shows the results of similar regression analyses for U.S. Senate and U.S. House elections. Each of the campaign cost variables is measured on a per voting age citizen basis. State geographic size is measured in units of 10,000 square miles. Personal income is measured in $1,000 units per voting age citizen.

The regression results shown in table 3.6 indicate that, once one controls for the importance of population, the cost of U.S. Senate elections and U.S. House elections are affected by geographic size and personal income (per voting age citizen) in a manner similar to that seen in gubernatorial elections. The geographic size of a state has a positive and statistically significant affect on the statewide per voter cost of U.S. House and senior senatorial elections. Personal income per voting age citizen has no statistically significant effect on the cost of either U.S. House elections or U.S. Senate elections.

It is unclear why the per voting age citizen wealth of a state does not seem to affect the per voter cost of gubernatorial, U.S. Senate, or U.S. House elections.[27] It may simply be that concentrations of wealth among individuals capable of contributing large sums of money are what is important to the cost of elections. However, such speculation is beyond the purpose of this text. What is important to recognize is that two factors do seem important to consider when evaluating the statewide cost of all three types of elections: population size and geographic size. And, even though these two factors are important to the cost

Table 3.6 Regressions of Campaign Costs per Voting Age Citizen of U.S. Senior Senator, U.S. Junior Senator, and U.S. Representative Elections, 1992–98.

| Variable | Senior Senator | Junior Senator | U.S. Representative |
|---|---|---|---|
| Intercept | −2.63 | 5.83* | .99 |
| State Geographic Size | .32* | .04 | .11* |
| Personal Income | .30 | −.17 | .08 |
| Total N | 69 | 93 | 101 |
| R-squared | .19 | .03 | .09 |

*Unstandardized regression coefficient is statistically significant at the .01 level.

considerations of all three types of elections, when it comes to cost per voting age citizen, gubernatorial elections appear to be different from U.S. Senate and House elections.[28] After controlling for the effect of population size (table 3.5), there is no statistically significant correlation between the per voting age citizen cost of gubernatorial elections and that of U.S. Senate and House elections. As such, while factors often considered important in affecting the cost of U.S. Senate and U.S. House elections might be important in gubernatorial elections, their importance in gubernatorial elections remains an open question.

## CONCLUSIONS

In this chapter, we examined the basic parameters of spending in gubernatorial elections. It was shown that, like the cost of U.S. Senate and U.S. House elections, the cost of gubernatorial elections rose well in excess of the inflation rate for the period of 1978 to 1998. It was also shown that spending in gubernatorial elections is highly related, on average, to statewide spending in U.S. Senate and U.S. House elections.

The data presented in this chapter suggest that a state's voting age population and geographic size are two important factors that condition the cost of gubernatorial elections. Once one controls for the effect of a state's voting age population, the cost of gubernatorial elections is not related to the cost of U.S. Senate and U.S. House elections. The importance of geographic size and personal income to the cost of gubernatorial elections is similar to their importance in U.S. Senate and U.S. House elections, at least when one controls for the influence of population. Geographic size generally has a positive and statistically significant effect on the cost per voting age citizen in gubernatorial, U.S. Senate, and U.S. House elections.[29]

The results in this chapter suggest two important points. First, it is important to control for the effect of population when trying to evaluate the cost of gubernatorial elections. Second, while previous research on the cost of U.S. Senate and U.S. House elections may help guide research on the cost of gubernatorial elections, there is simply no assurance that the factors that are important in affecting the cost of U.S. Senate and U.S. House elections will be as important in gubernatorial elections. The importance of political factors in general, and campaign finance proposals in particular, to the cost of gubernatorial campaigns is clearly an open empirical question. It is the importance of these factors that we examine in the next chapter.

# CHAPTER 4

# Explaining Candidate Spending in Gubernatorial Elections

Costs of gubernatorial elections have risen over the last twenty years, even when controlling for the effects of inflation, and, unless there are significant changes in the current system of campaign finance, there is every reason to suspect that costs will continue to climb for the foreseeable future. Concern over the growing costs of electoral campaigns often fuels the call for campaign reform, even though it is unclear what types of fundamental change would either reduce the costs of elections or reduce the growth in the costs of elections.[1]

In their extensive overview of state campaign finance laws, Michael Malbin and Thomas Gais suggest that little can be said with certainty regarding the electoral consequences of campaign finance laws.[2] In a similar vein, Malcolm Jewell and William Cassie, writing the conclusion for the most exhaustive study of state legislative campaign finance to date, observe that there is not enough evidence "to conclude that public financing would succeed or fail in meeting the goals of reformers."[3] Works studying the effects of reform at the national level have provided contradictory, and often controversial, assessments regarding the electoral consequences of campaign finance laws. While some emphasize the negative consequences of reform, others provide a more positive evaluation.[4]

In this chapter, we address the issue of campaign costs in gubernatorial elections. While the previous chapter suggested that nonpolitical factors, population size and geographic size, condition the costs of elections, in this chapter we estimate the importance of political factors to the cost of gubernatorial elections. In particular, we address the question of how contribution limits, spending limits, and public financing provisions affect the cost of gubernatorial elections. We begin by examining some simple cost comparisons between those states that have adopted campaign reform proposals and those that have not adopted them. We then consider a multivariate model of campaign costs in gubernatorial elections that involves both campaign reform factors and other political factors that have often been shown to affect the costs of elections in the United States. We also consider whether or not there are clear partisan differences in how reform proposals affect the cost of gubernatorial elections and how incumbent spending is affected by these proposals.

## CAMPAIGN COSTS AND FINANCE REFORM PROPOSALS: A FIRST LOOK

As we discussed in chapter 2, the adoption of campaign finance reform proposals has been a slow evolutionary process across the states. Even as we write this book, some very large states, such as Texas and Illinois, place few restrictions on contributions to candidates for the governorship and provide no public funding to candidates while other states have a large number of restrictions on contributions, provide public subsidies to gubernatorial candidates, and place expenditure limits on those candidates who accept public subsidies. The combinations of finance reform measures that specific states have adopted have also changed over the time period, 1978 to 1998, that we are examining in this text. It is, of course, the variations in campaign finance law over the time period and across the states that make state gubernatorial elections such excellent natural laboratories in which to analyze the effects of campaign finance laws.

Table 4.1 shows the percentage of all gubernatorial races in our data set that have different types of campaign finance provisions.[5] As can be seen in table 4.1, almost 17 percent of gubernatorial elections had some form of public financing to candidates, while in a little over 20 percent of the cases there was some form

**Table 4.1** Percentage of All Gubernatorial Races with Spending Limits, Public Financing Provisions, and Contribution Limits, 1978–98

| Campaign Finance Regulation | Races with Regulation (%) | (N) |
|---|---|---|
| Spending Limits | 13.6 | (41) |
| Public Financing to Parties | 20.5 | (62) |
| Public Financing to Candidates | 16.9 | (51) |
| Contributions Limits | | |
|     Corporations | 72.2 | (218) |
|     Unions | 62.6 | (189) |
|     Individuals | 57.0 | (172) |
|     PACs | 46.0 | (139) |
|     Family Members | 38.7 | (117) |
|     Candidates | 8.6 | (26) |

of public financing to political parties. In about 14 percent of the cases, there were spending limits. One important consideration in these figures is that, because of U.S. Supreme Court decisions, spending limits are almost always directly tied to the public financing of candidates.[6] Because of this linkage, it is extremely difficult to specify the effects of spending limits independent of a consideration of public financing to candidates.

When it comes to contribution limits, as can be seen in table 4.1, the most common type of restriction involves limitations on corporate contributions, followed by those on unions, individuals, PACs, family members, and candidates. It should be noted that, because contributions from corporations and unions are most likely to be perceived as tainted, they are also mostly likely to be prohibited. The data in table 4.1 do not reflect differences in the amount of contribution limits that may exist among the states. For example, is the limit on individual contributions set at $500 or $1,000? Nevertheless, there does appear to be a cumulative property of restrictiveness underlying the contribution data shown in table 4.1. In the 26 cases where there were restrictions on candidates, there also were always restrictions on family members, individuals, unions, and corporations. In only one case was there a restriction on candidates but not on PACs. As such, the data on contribution limits that were used to create the information in table 4.1 can also be used to create a unidimensional cumulative scale indicating the restrictiveness of a state's system of contribution limits in a given year. Each state is coded 1 if it imposed a particular type of limit and 0 if it had no limits. Each state's score on each of the six types of contribution limits is then added together to create a scale from 0 to 6. A state that has the most restrictive contribution system, a score of 6, utilizes all six types of the contribution limits, while a state that imposes none of the contribution limits listed in table 4.1 has a score of 0 and is the least restrictive.[7] The percentages of states in the seven categories, from least restrictive, 0, to most restrictive, 6, are 27.5 percent, 7.3 percent, 8.3 percent, 7.6 percent, 16.6 percent, 24.5 percent, and 8.3 percent, respectively.

The question remains, though: are contribution limits, spending limits, and public financing effective means to reduce the cost of gubernatorial elections? The information given in table 4.2 provides some initial answers to this question. When it comes to contribution limits, the evidence seems quite clear: states that have contribution limits do not, on average, have less expensive gubernatorial elections. In fact, it appears that states that have contribution limits spend, on average, more than states that do not have contribution limits. In four of the six cases (limits on individual, PAC, family member, and candidate contributions), there is a statistically significant difference, .05, between the mean level of spending in states with a given contribution limit and states without the limit.

If one considers the scale of contribution restrictiveness discussed above, it again appears that a more restrictive environment results in higher average

**Table 4.2** Mean Spending per Voting Age Citizen in Gubernatorial Elections and the Absence or Presence of Campaign Finance Regulations

| Campaign Finance Regulation | Mean Level of Spending | |
|---|---|---|
| | Absence of Regulation | Presence of Regulation |
| Corporation Contribution Limits | 2.94 | 3.47 |
| Union Contribution Limits | 2.93 | 3.56 |
| Individual Contribution Limits* | 2.83 | 3.70 |
| PAC Contribution Limits* | 2.82 | 3.92 |
| Family Member Contribution Limits* | 2.82 | 4.12 |
| Candidate Contribution Limits* | 3.21 | 4.60 |
| Public Financing to Parties | 3.24 | 3.65 |
| Public Financing to Candidates | 3.38 | 3.09 |
| Spending Limits | 3.40 | 3.03 |

*Difference in the Means is statistically significant at the .05 level.

spending in gubernatorial elections. The correlation between the state scale scores and state spending per voting age citizen is a positive 0.16, which is statistically significant at the .01 level. States that have the least restrictive environments (scores of 0 and 1) have mean spending per voting age citizen values of 2.96 and 3.27, respectively, while the states with the most restrictive environments (scores of 5 and 6) have the highest mean scores with values of 4.4 and 4.69, respectively. These correlations suggest that states with more restrictive environments for contributions actually tend to spend more on a per voting age citizen basis than states with less restrictive environments. So, the evidence seems to support the conclusion that contribution limits do not limit the level of per voting age citizen spending by candidates.

If we turn our attention to the issues of public financing and spending limits, the evidence given in table 4.2 is much less definitive. States that provide public funding to political parties tend to have more expensive gubernatorial elections than those that do not provide public financing. On the other hand, states that have spending limits and states that provide public financing to candidates tend, on average, to have less expensive gubernatorial elections. But none of these differences in means are statistically significant at the .05 level. In addition, the presence of spending limits is not really independent of public financing to candidates because spending limits almost always exist with public funding of candidates. As such, there is no statistical basis at this time to support the proposition that public financing of political parties, public funding of candidates, or spending limits significantly affect the average cost of gubernatorial elections.

Now it might be argued that the evidence in table 4.2 is problematic because it is based upon whether or not a state has a given type of campaign finance provision and does not take into consideration the actual dollar amount attached to that provision. For example, the data do not distinguish between states that have a contribution limit of $500 and those that have a limit of $1,000 or more. The actual level at which particular contribution limits are set may affect a campaign's ability to raise money and consequently its spending coffers. It may simply be more difficult to raise large sums of money when contribution limits are set at $500 instead of $1,000 or more, and so there is less money to spend.

It is inherently more difficult to analyze the relationship between limit levels of campaign finance provisions and campaign expenditures. One could focus an analysis on only those states for given years that have contribution limits and then examine the relationship between given contribution limit levels and per voter expenditures. The difficulty with this approach is that one necessarily is dealing with much smaller subsets of the data, which may not necessarily be representative of all states in general. An alternative approach would be to assign all states that do not have a particular type of contribution limit an arbitrarily high value as a contribution limit. One can then analyze the relationship between spending limits and per voting age citizen expenditures for the entire data set. Of course, the difficulty with this approach is that any value assigned to states that do not have a particular type of contribution limit is necessarily arbitrary. We have elected to utilize both approaches.

Table 4.3 portrays the correlations between total per voting age citizen spending in gubernatorial elections and the levels of contribution limits for the period of 1978 to 1998. The correlations in column one are based upon those states that have actual contribution limits. The correlations in column two are based upon an analysis of all states where those states that did not actually have contribution limits were assigned a limit of $1 million. Once again, the data indicate that contribution limits do not reduce the per voting age citizen cost of running gubernatorial elections. None of the correlations in column one are statistically significant. While four of the six correlations in column two are

**Table 4.3** Correlations Between Spending per Voting Age Citizen in Gubernatorial Elections and Levels of Contributions Limits: All States and States with Actual Contribution Limits, 1978–98

| Type of Contribution Limit | Per Voting Age Citizen Spending in Gubernatorial Elections | |
| --- | --- | --- |
| | States with Actual Contribution Limits | All States |
| Corporation | .05 (218) | −.08 |
| Union | −.07 (189) | −.09 |
| Individual | −.12 (172) | −.13* |
| PAC | −.13 (139) | −.17* |
| Family Member | −.15 (117) | −.20* |
| Candidate | −.32 (26) | −.12* |

*Figure is statistically significant at the .05 level.

statistically significant at the .05 level, they are all in the opposite direction hypothesized. In fact, 11 of the 12 correlations are negative and the only one that is positive is very small and statistically insignificant. If there is any conclusion to be drawn from table 4.3, it is that states that have lower contribution limits tend to have higher per voting age citizen costs in gubernatorial elections.[8]

As stated earlier in this book, advocates of campaign contribution limits often argue that contribution limits can achieve a number of desirable ends. They can eliminate the "fat cat" contributor, they can lower the costs of elections, and they can democratize the contribution system. While we do not have the data on gubernatorial elections to analyze the first and third of these claims, the evidence presented so far clearly suggests that contribution laws simply *do not,* on average, reduce the total per voting age citizen cost of gubernatorial elections. For some, this finding may not be particularly surprising. Malbin and Gais, for example, argue that, in the context of political parties, contribution limits do not work simply because potential contributors readily find ways to circumvent the law.[9]

While proponents of contribution limits continue to argue that limits can reduce the cost of elections,[10] opponents of strict contribution limits argue that they can seriously inhibit the ability of candidates to raise money. At the federal level, individual contribution limits were, in fact, raised from $1,000 to $2,000 in the campaign finance reform act passed in 2002 largely in response to this argument. Our data cannot directly answer how difficult campaign fundraising becomes under a system of strict contribution limits. It may be more difficult to get a thousand $1,000 contribution than one $100,000 contribution. But we can clearly state that contribution limits do not appear to lower the average total cost of gubernatorial elections.

When it comes to public financing and spending limits, this initial analysis is simply not definitive. We found no statistically significant results when comparing the average per voting age citizen cost in states with these reform laws as compared to those states without such laws. Of course, if most candidates accept public financing and associated spending limits, in those states where there are spending limits, there is going to be a relationship between the level of the spending limit and the total cost of the associated gubernatorial election. But such a conclusion is trivial.

To this point our analyses have been relatively straightforward: simple comparisons of means and correlations. It is well known that such simplified comparisons can be problematic when analyzing fairly complex phenomena such as campaign spending. Important relationships can remain hidden or even falsely identified when there are intricate relationships among all of the variables of interest. Therefore, in the next section of this chapter we consider a multivariate regression model of spending in gubernatorial elections. This model will allow us to identify the importance of a number of characteristics that affect the cost of gubernatorial elections and to more properly understand the role of campaign finance regulations. We will also be able to examine if campaign finance regulations have a systematic partisan bias or a bias in favor of incumbents.

## CAMPAIGN COSTS IN GUBERNATORIAL ELECTIONS: MULTIVARIATE MODELS

Numerous political considerations can affect the cost of elections in the United States. Earlier in this text we briefly discussed the 1999 Kentucky gubernatorial election where numerous political forces sharply reduced the overall cost of the election and negated the potential significance of the campaign reform law. We begin this section, therefore, with a brief discussion of a number of political factors that can be seen as likely to affect the cost of gubernatorial elections. We then use a multivariate regression model to examine the importance of these political factors and campaign finance reform laws to the total cost of gubernatorial elections. We also examine if there are clear partisan differences in the consequences of campaign finance laws. We conclude by using a similar multivariate model to specify whether or not campaign finance reform laws affect the campaign costs of incumbents and challengers in a similar manner.

By definition, the total cost of a campaign includes spending in both the primary season and the general election period by both winners and losers. One political characteristic that can affect the total cost of a state's gubernatorial election is the absence or presence of a financially competitive primary season. A large number of states do not distinguish between spending in the primary season and spending during the general election. Thus, we cannot analyze spending during just the general election season for much of our data set. We can, however, examine the impact of total spending by the losing candidates in the Democratic and Republican primaries. It can be hypothesized, therefore, that the spending per voting age citizen by the losing candidates in the Democratic and Republican primaries will have a positive effect upon a state's total per voting age citizen cost of its gubernatorial election. Spending has a direct effect in that it not only adds to the overall measure of costs but also forces the eventual nominee to expend funds to obtain the nomination. If the eventual nominee does not face serious competition in the primary, it is not likely that he or she will spend large sums of money during the primary season.[11]

Incumbency is a second political variable that must be considered when evaluating the cost of gubernatorial elections. It is not immediately clear whether the presence of an incumbent necessarily increases or decreases the total cost of a gubernatorial election. Incumbents in American elections are generally able to raise large amounts of money; but they may also scare off serious opponents, which likely reduces the total cost of an election.[12] Nevertheless, it is important to consider incumbency when evaluating partisan differences in spending. It has been well documented that in American elections incumbents are generally able to outspend challengers.[13] It can be hypothesized, therefore, that the presence of a Democratic gubernatorial incumbent ought to increase total Democratic spending and decrease total Republican spending. Likewise, the presence of a Republican gubernatorial incumbent ought to increase total Republican spending and decrease total Democratic spending. One might also suspect that an election will have two financially competitive candidates when there is an open seat with no incumbent running.

A third political characteristic that is important to consider is competition. It is generally argued that more competitive elections tend, on average, to be more expensive.[14] In this analysis we use two measures of competition. One we actually call *competition*. Competition is a general measure of the overall competitive environment in the state independent of the particular gubernatorial election. It takes into account the average level of inter-party competitiveness based upon electoral outcomes in the state's most recent presidential election, two most recent U.S. Senate elections, and partisan percentages in the state senate and state house.[15] Our second measure we call *margin*. Margin is defined as the absolute value of one major party nominee's vote in the general election minus the other major party nominee's vote in the general election. It is, in effect, a measure of the competition in the actual gubernatorial election of interest.

The final political characteristic that we consider is often referred to as the "electoral context."[16] The electoral context consists of a series of political factors that can affect spending and electoral outcomes that are not readily measurable. Examples of such factors include whether in a given year there appeared to be a nationwide pro-Democratic movement or whether there was an anti-incumbency mood. To control for the electoral context, we include dummy variables for each of the years included in the analyses.[17]

Any multivariate regression model that attempts to examine the cost of gubernatorial elections must include the political variables discussed above. Likewise, the geographic variables discussed in chapter 3 must also be included as control variables. Because the focus of this book is on campaign finance reform, we also include four campaign finance reform variables in our multivariate regression models. One we include is the unidimensional cumulative scale of a state's system of contribution limits that was discussed earlier in this chapter. As stated, the scale ranges from 0 to 6 and can be viewed in terms of a state's overall restrictiveness. Low scores indicate few or no limits on campaign contributions while high scores indicate numerous limits.

Of course, this scale does not reflect the differences that may exist among the states having a particular type of contribution limit. For example, is the limit on individual contributions set at $500 or $1,000? However, three important considerations lead us to utilize this particular measurement. First, in terms of an individual's or group's potential to contribute a total number of dollars, the differences among the states that limit a potential type of contribution is small compared to the differences between those states that limit a potential type of contribution and those that do not establish a limit. In ANOVA terminology, the between category variance is much greater than the within category variance. Second, the inclusion of all six contribution limit variables separately would have created a number of methodological problems, including sever multicolinearity.[18] Finally, from a theoretical perspective, the overall regulatory environment is more important to potential contributors and candidates than the specific level of any particular contribution limit. So, for example, if a state does not limit PAC contributions, it makes little difference to a corporation or union whether a state places a $500 limit on corporate/union contributions or prohibits such contributions altogether because they can filter money to a candidate through political action committees.[19]

To measure public financing, we created two dummy variables. The first is coded 1 if the state provided public funding directly to candidates, and is coded 0 otherwise. The second is coded 1 if the state provided public funding to political parties, 0 otherwise. Finally, to measure spending limits, we include a variable indicating the level of the spending limit on a per citizen basis for those states that imposed limits. Those states that did not have spending limits were given a score of 0. Since spending limits are inevitably entwined with candidate-based public financing, this measure has to be interpreted within the context of the candidate-based public financing dummy variable. The candidate-based public financing variable should indicate the change in the intercept of the regression equation that results from a state having spending limits, while the spending limits variable acts as an interactive effect, indicating the effect of the level of the limits for those states that have spending limits.

Table 4.4 portrays the results of a series of multivariate regression models that examine the importance of political factors, geographic factors, and campaign finance reform measures to different cost considerations of gubernatorial elections.[20] As can be seen in column one, the geographic variables affect the total cost per voting age citizen of gubernatorial elections in much the same way as shown in chapter 3. The geographic size variable has a positive and statistically significant effect on cost while the per capita income variable effect is statistically insignificant. If we turn our attention to the political variables, spending by the losing candidates in the Democratic primary and in the Republican primary behave much as expected. Both have a positive and statistically significant effect on total cost. The margin variable also behaves as expected; it is negative and statistically significant. The closer the margin, the higher the total cost of the election. The competition variable, however, is positive and statistically significant; just the opposite of what one would expect. While this finding is somewhat counterintuitive, candidate spending may serve as a means of compensating for an unfavorable party balance. Finally, the absence or presence of an incumbent does not have a statistically significant impact on the total cost of gubernatorial elections.[21]

In line with the results presented earlier in this chapter, it appears that states that have more stringent contribution limits do not have less expensive gubernatorial elections. The coefficient in table 4.4 associated with the contribution limit index is positive and statistically significant. It appears that having more stringent contribution limits actually increases the per voting age citizen cost of gubernatorial elections. Notably, public funding to political parties has no statistically significant effect on total costs.

What can states do to affect total spending in gubernatorial elections? For one thing, they can provide a combination of candidate-based public financing and spending limits. To gauge the effects of reform, one has to look both at the coefficient for the variable indicating whether a state provided candidate-based public financing and the coefficient for the variable indicating the effect of spending limits on a per voting age citizen basis. As seen in table 4.4, both are statistically significant.[22] Overall, the effects of such reforms depend greatly on the level of any associated spending limits. For example, in an election with candidate-based public financing and spending limits set at $.50 per voting age citizen, total spending would be expected to decrease, on average, by approximately $.05. With limits set at a $1.00 per voting age citizen, however, total spending would be expected to increase by approximately $.64. Very simply, approximately $.54 per voting age citizen appears to be the break-even point so that spending limits above this point tend to increase total per voting age citizen gubernatorial spending, with limits below this point tending to decrease overall spending.

If we turn our attention to the second and third columns in table 4.4, we see that the geographic and political variables generally behave much as we would expect them to operate in regards to party spending.[23] Geographic size has a positive and statistically significant effect on Democratic and Republican spending, while per capita income has no statistically significant effect. Higher spending by the losing candidates in the Democratic primary increases overall Democratic spending, while higher spending by the losing candidates in the Republican primary increases overall Republican spending. Margin and competition behave much as they do when considering total spending. And the presence of a Democratic incumbent tends to increase Democratic spending, while the presence of a Republican incumbent tends to increase Republican spending. It is interesting to note, however, that the presence of a Democratic incumbent tends to decrease Republican spending while the presence of a Republican

**Table 4.4** Regressions of Gubernatorial Candidate Spending per Voting Age Citizen, Campaign Finance Regulations, Geographic Variables, and Political Variables, 1978–98

| Variable | Total Spending | Democratic Spending | Republican Spending | Incumbent Spending | Challenger Spending |
|---|---|---|---|---|---|
| Margin | −.025 (.009)*** | −.011 (.006)** | −.014 (.003)*** | −.011 (.007)* | −.014 (.005)*** |
| Competition | .024 (.009)** | .018 (.006)*** | .007 (.003)** | .016 (.009)* | .012 (.004)*** |
| Incumbent Seeking Reelection | −.074 (.239) | | | | |
| Democratic Incumbent | | .416 (.176)** | −.429 (.108)*** | −.115 (.157) | −.198 (.112)* |
| Republican Incumbent | | .111 (.169) | .181 (.108)* | | |
| Spending by Losing Candidates in Democratic/incumbent Primary | 1.751 (.249)*** | .536 (.168)*** | | .285 (.517) | |
| Spending by losing Candidates in Republican/Challenger Primary | .962 (.290)*** | | .206 (.080)** | | .318 (.162)** |

| | | | | | |
|---|---|---|---|---|---|
| Size of State in Square Miles | .141(.032)*** | .050 (.013)*** | .047 (.008)*** | .047 (.014)*** | .024 (.011)** |
| Per Capita Income | –.026 (.015) | –.010 (.006) | –.007 (.004) | –.007 | –.002 (.007) |
| Contribution Limits index | .148 (.063)** | .065 (.041) | .017 (.022) | .106 (.057)* | .017 (.030) |
| Public Financing to Parties | .303 (.248) | .104 (.157) | .020 (.101) | .010 (.250) | .281 (.160) |
| Candidate Financing | –.758 (.287)*** | –.407 (.176)** | –.254 (.121)** | –.539 (.290)* | –.155 (.157) |
| Spending Limits per Voting Age Citizen | 1.404 (.515)*** | .845 (.296)*** | .358 (.210)* | 1.10 (.420)*** | .254 (.249) |
| Constant | 1.085 (.492)** | .283 (.263) | .819 (.176)*** | .575 (.261)** | .635 (.210)*** |
| R-squared | .72 | .37 | .48 | .26 | .45 |

Note: For the purposes of presentation, year variables are not included in the table. Standard errors are in parentheses. $^*p < .10$, $^{**}p < .05$, $^{***}p < .01$.

incumbent has no statistically significant effect on Democratic spending. It may be surmised that Democratic incumbents are more successful in scaring off financially viable challengers than their Republican counterparts.

Do campaign finance reforms have a partisan effect? When it comes to contribution limits and the public financing of political parties, the answer appears to be no. The coefficients are positive in all cases, but none are statistically significant. Spending limits do appear to have potential partisan implications, and these implications are much like what one would expect. While the direction and significance of the coefficients are the same for both parties, Republican, rather than Democratic, spending is more likely to be affected negatively by the imposition of spending limits. In this respect, Republican spending would be expected to decline by $.07 under a $.50 per voting age citizen limit and increase by only $.11 under a $1.00 per citizen limit. Democrats would see their spending increase by $.02 under a $.50 per citizen limit and by $.44 under a $1.00 per citizen limit. At least when one considers the entire time period of 1978 to 1998, Democrats seem to fare better than Republicans in states that have candidate-based public financing and spending limits. Of course, the results in table 4.4 may reflect the fact that fewer Republicans choose to participate in public financing and the associated spending limits. As fewer candidates participate, actual spending becomes increasingly disassociated from spending limits.[24] At the one extreme, if no candidate accepts public financing, spending limits will have little or no effect on actual spending. At the other extreme, if all candidates are coerced into accepting public financing and spending limits, the effect of reform efforts will be maximized.

As in most American elections, incumbents in gubernatorial races have an overall advantage. The financial advantage of incumbency is well documented as is concern that campaign finance laws may have a differential effect on incumbents as opposed to challengers.[25] Columns four and five of table 4.4 show the results of a series of regression analyses that examine the effects of geographic variables, political variables, and campaign finance reform variables on incumbent spending and challenger spending, respectively.[26] With the exception that spending by losing candidates in the incumbent's primary has no significant effect on incumbent spending, the political and geographic variables behave much as we have come to expect. Likewise, public financing to political parties has no significant effect on either incumbent or challenger spending.

The contribution limit index is interesting in that the results support neither the arguments of proponents nor the fears of opponents. Opponents of reform often argue that contribution limits make it difficult for challengers to raise money when they face incumbents. But the coefficient in column five is positive and statistically insignificant. It appears that a more stringent regulatory environment does not make it more difficult for challengers to raise money. If one considers all of the coefficients associated with the contribution limit index, there is simply no evidence to suggest that a more stringent regulatory environment can work to reduce campaign costs. Nor does challenger spending seem to be significantly affected by candidate financing or spending limits. At least in the case of gubernatorial elections, our evidence suggests that public funding to candidates does not seem to encourage challenger spending.

While campaign finance reform is often intended to control the expense of election campaigns, it is also intended to reduce the differential in candidate spending. In order to investigate this possibility, we specified the difference in candidate spending by taking the absolute value of the difference in Republican and Democratic spending per voting age citizen. The difference in spending was then regressed on the state campaign finance provisions as well as the various political and geographical variables utilized throughout most of this chapter. The results of this analysis are shown in table 4.5.[27]

As can be seen in table 4.5, the difference in candidate spending is affected by both spending limits (in combination with candidate-based public financing) and contribution limits. In this respect, spending limits generally work to reduce the disparity in candidate spending, though effect is contingent on the level of the spending limit. For example, with spending limits set at $.50 per voting age citizen, the difference in candidate spending would be reduced by about $.35 per citizen. With limits set at a $1.00 per voting age citizen, the difference in spending would increase by approximately $.04. Contribution limits also affect absolute differences in spending, but they do so by increasing rather than decreasing differences in candidate spending. In states that restrict each category of contributions, the difference in spending would, on average, be $.54 higher than in states without any contribution limits.

## CONCLUSIONS

In this chapter, we examined how campaign finance reform measures affect various cost considerations in gubernatorial elections. We began with a number of relatively straightforward and simple analyses and then moved to a series of multivariate considerations. Beyond campaign finance reform measures, we also examined the importance of a number of geographic and political variables to cost considerations.

In terms of geographic considerations, the geographic size, measured in square miles, of a state had a positive and statistically significant effect on cost whether one looks at total spending, Democratic spending, Republican spending, incumbent spending, or challenger spending. Conversely, per capita income never had a statistically significant effect on cost. In most cases, political variables operated as expected. In all cases, the closer the margin of the election, the

**Table 4.5** Regression of Spending Difference on State Campaign Finance
Regulations, Gubernatorial Elections, 1978–98

| Variable | Absolute Spending Difference |
|---|---|
| Margin | .007 (.005) |
| Competition | .010 (.006)* |
| Incumbent Seeking Re-Election | −.201 (.132) |
| Size of State (Square Miles) | .012 (.009) |
| Per Capita Income | −.007 (.005) |
| Spending By Losing Candidates in Democratic Primary | .107 (.146) |
| Spending By Losing Candidates in Republican Primary | .057 (.089) |
| Candidate Financing | −.347 (.152)** |
| Spending Limits Per Voting Age Citizen | .390 (.260)* |
| Contribution Limits | .082 (.035)** |
| Public Financing To Parties | −.001 (.124) |
| Constant | .177 (.193) |
| R- squared | .18 |

Note: For the purpose of presentation, year variables are not included in the
table. Standard errors are in parentheses. * $p < .1$; ** $p < .05$.

higher the cost of the election. While the presence of an incumbent by itself did
not seem to affect total spending, the presence of a Democratic incumbent
tended to increase Democratic spending and the presence of a Republican
incumbent tended to increase Republican spending. And, with the exception of
incumbent spending, the higher the spending by losing candidates in a primary,
the higher the spending by the eventual nominee.

When it comes to contribution limits, it appears they do not reduce the per
voting age citizen cost of gubernatorial elections. Contribution limits may make
it more difficult for candidates to raise money, but they do not stop candidates
from collecting it. This observation is true whether one looks at a simple comparison of means, as we did in the first part of this chapter, or at more complex

multivariate models. It is also true if one considers total spending, Democratic spending, Republican spending, incumbent spending, or challenger spending. If anything, states that have more restrictive contribution limits tend, on average, to have higher levels of spending. Proponents of contribution limits can take heart in the fact that a more stringent regulatory environment does not appear to limit the ability of challengers to raise money as is often claimed by opponents of restrictive limits. Of course, a more stringent regulatory environment did seem to increase the difference in spending between candidates. Thus, contribution limits must be justified on some basis other than as a cost control mechanism.

Public funding to political parties does not seem to have any significant effect on the cost of elections. While the average per voting age citizen total cost of gubernatorial elections is higher in states where there is public funding to political parties compared to states without public funding, the difference is not statistically significant. Thus, Malbin and Gais appear correct when they assert that the public funding of political parties is generally not enough to make a significant difference in the role of political parties.[28]

If states want to institute mechanisms to control campaign costs, our analyses indicate that public financing with spending limits can be an effective tool to control the cost of gubernatorial elections. Of course, cost control depends upon two major considerations. First, the specification of the actual spending limit is important. However, at this time we cannot state what an "ideal" spending limit might be. Second, steps must be taken to encourage candidates to abide by the spending limits. Unless there are inducements or other mechanisms to gain compliance, public financing and spending limits will eventually fail as cost containment mechanisms.

As shown in table 4.5, public financing of candidates, along with spending limits, can be used to reduce the differential in candidate spending. Leveling the playing field has long been a goal of campaign finance reformers. The importance of a level playing field, however, needs to be viewed in the context of what is often seen as a central characteristic of a viable democracy: electoral competition. In this sense, financial equity among candidates is not necessarily a goal in itself. Its importance lies in its theoretical linkage to a competitive political environment. All other things being equal, reformers hope that by equalizing candidate spending greater electoral competition will be achieved.[29] It is the linkage between campaign finance reform and electoral competition that we consider in the next chapter.

# CHAPTER 5

## State Campaign Finance and Electoral Competition

In the previous two chapters, we investigated the direct effects of campaign finance regulation on candidate campaign spending. But from a normative standpoint, we are less interested in campaign spending for its own sake than for the potential distorting impact it may have on elections specifically and democracy more broadly. As Herbert Alexander notes, there are no absolute standards for judging whether campaign spending is too high or too low.[1] Besides, the question we most want answered is not whether too much (or too little) is being spent in the quest for elective office, but whether campaigns are significantly better (or worse) because of this spending. Are elections more competitive in higher spending campaigns? Are citizens more or less involved? Are they more or less informed?

In this chapter, we investigate the impact of campaign spending on electoral competition, as well as the impact, both direct and indirect, of campaign finance regulations on competition. Before doing so, we should acknowledge that we approach the question from a certain normative point of view: That is, we believe that competitive participatory elections are a sign of a healthy democracy. There are, of course, reasons to believe just the opposite—that competitive elections are more indicative of an inherent instability in the political system than of a robust democracy at play. Consider, for example, the 2000 presidential election, which was so close that the legitimacy of the eventual outcome remains in doubt even today. A slew of editorials following the election raised the question of whether we—as a nation—have become too divided to govern. Regardless of how one answers the question, it is easy to see that competitive hard-fought elections may create as many problems with respect to the legitimacy of a political system as they solve.

Likewise, high voter participation may be a sign of a vibrant democracy, but it may also be a sign of an angry mob whose dissatisfaction is targeted not just at the ruling party but at the political system as well. As James Madison knowingly wrote over 200 years ago, the greatest threat to a republican form of government comes not from a minority faction but from an impassioned majority hell-bent on depriving others of their individual rights.

Yet democracy—even in the relatively limited form envisioned by Madison—is predicated on the notion that voters should have a voice, albeit a heavily filtered one, in the selection of their rulers. More evolved though still fairly minimalist visions of democracy assume citizens will not only have the ability to "throw the bums out" but will also, at least occasionally, be compelled to action. Free and fair elections, and the competition that such elections generate, become the means to this end. To be truly democratic, the choice between competing elites must be real and not merely a facade in which elections provide the illusion of public control. Unfortunately, whether U.S. gubernatorial elections provide meaningful choices is a complex problem that cannot be fully examined within the current context. We can, however, explore the nature of electoral competition in gubernatorial elections.

## COMPETITION IN GUBERNATORIAL ELECTIONS

In order for elections to be competitive, the ruling incumbent or party must be somewhat vulnerable. Vote margins, which indicate the gap between the votes received by winner and loser in an election, provide a natural starting point for investigating vulnerability in gubernatorial elections. Figure 5.1 presents the average margin of victory for winning gubernatorial candidates from 1978 to 1998.[2] As can be seen in the chart, with the exception of spikes in 1992 and 1996, electoral competition in gubernatorial elections has remained remarkably stable. Because most states hold gubernatorial elections during presidential midterms, we should resist the temptation to conclude the spikes show a trend toward declining competition. More likely, the apparent jump in electoral margin observed in 1992 and 1996 are short-term blips. But even if they are not, we lack the evidence to conclude that they are indicative of a broader trend. The overall pattern appears, at best, a slight trend toward larger gubernatorial margins of victory within an environment of remarkably stable competition.

While the margin of victory gives us some insight into gubernatorial competition, it does not inform us about patterns of partisanship or incumbent vulnerability. For this we turn to the average incumbent and Democratic vote percentages presented in figure 5.2. Looking at figure 5.2, a couple of patterns emerge. First, at least in terms of average shares of the vote, incumbent governors were more successful in the 1990s. However, their success did not necessarily mean they were

**Figure 5.1** Average Margin of Victory in Gubernatorial Elections, 1978–98

less vulnerable to electoral challenge. From 1990 to 1993, the number of incumbents defeated increased along with the average margin of victory of incumbents. After 1993, incumbent reelection rates began to climb, matching the increase in electoral margins. Second, as in Congress and state legislatures, Democrats lost control of governors' mansions during the 1990s, which is illustrated in figure 5.2 by the declining average Democratic percentage of the two-party vote. The Democrats won approximately 59 percent of the gubernatorial elections from 1978 to 1989, but only approximately 44 percent of the elections from 1990 to 1998.

The overall increases in campaign spending documented in chapter 3 have been associated with partisan change, but not with an overall increase in average electoral competition. Republicans have made gains; nevertheless, the average level of competition has remained virtually unchanged. In addition, because the standard deviation for each of these measures of competition has remained relatively stable, we have no reason to believe that gubernatorial elections have become more volatile, as Gary Jacobson has argued regarding congressional elections.[3]

The most vulnerable incumbents are, of course, those who are actually defeated. In gubernatorial elections from 1978 to 1998, roughly 20 percent of

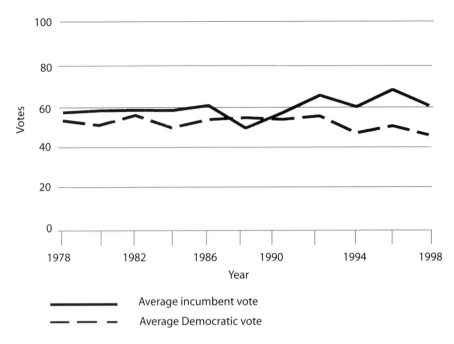

**Figure 5.2** Average Incumbent and Democratic Shares of the Gubernatorial Election Vote by Percentage, 1978–98

gubernatorial incumbents lost their bid for reelection. In this sense, gubernatorial elections are more competitive than U.S. House elections, but fairly similar to U.S. Senate elections. And though there is some variation across four-year election cycles (see table 5.1), as in other types of elections, there is a clear and persistent incumbency advantage. Certain factors do moderate the advantage. Notably (looking at table 5.1), incumbent success rates were lowest during the early 1990s when states were confronted with the double whammy of declining federal dollars and shrinking general revenues due to an economic recession. Governors during this period were placed in the unenviable role of either asking for tax increases or cutting government programs.[4] During the latter part of the 1990s, with states running budget surpluses and the economy thriving, incumbent governors faced much better prospects in their quests for reelection.

## EXPLAINING PATTERNS OF COMPETITION: THE IMPORTANCE OF MONEY

The most advantageous position for a candidate, aside from being an incumbent, is to be a candidate with money to spend. Put simply, the candidate who spends the most money generally—though not always—wins the race. In just under 72 percent of gubernatorial elections from 1978 to 1998, the candidate spending the

**Table 5.1** Incumbent Success Rates in Gubernatorial Elections, 1978–98

| Years | No. of Incumbents Seeking Reelection | No. of Winning Incumbents | Percentage of Winning Incumbents |
|---|---|---|---|
| 1978–81 | 32 | 24 | 75 |
| 1982–85 | 32 | 24 | 75 |
| 1986–89 | 26 | 22 | 85 |
| 1990–93 | 29 | 20 | 69 |
| 1994–97 | 31 | 26 | 84 |
| 1998* | 24 | 22 | 91 |

* One year only.

most money won the election. Although there are enough campaign fundraising losers–election winners to cast doubt on any deterministic relationship between spending and votes, there also are enough big spending winners to suggest that the odds-on favorite in any given election is the candidate spending the most money. In other words, money does not guarantee victory, but it certainly helps.

Money and incumbency combined create a synergy that is difficult even in the worst of times for challengers to overcome. From 1978 to 1998, 83.5 percent of winning incumbents outspent their opposition, while only 16.5 percent of winning incumbents were outspent by their opposition. Of the losing incumbents, 63 percent outspent their opponent, leaving 37 percent who were outspent. In open-seat elections, the candidate spending the most money won 69 percent of the time.

While outspending opponents was not quite as potent as incumbency, candidates who spent more than their opponent between 1978 and 1998, on average, received just under 56 percent of the two-party vote. Further, incumbents who were the top spending candidates received over 60 percent, while open-seat candidates who outspent their opposition won with 54 percent of the two-party vote.

Besides affecting who wins and who loses, money and incumbency are important in determining the closeness of a political race. In open-seat elections, the average Democratic candidate can expect to garner a bare majority of 51 percent of the two-party vote. Where a Democratic incumbent is running for reelection, the average Democratic vote rises to 60 percent. With an incumbent Republican running for reelection, the average Democratic vote falls to just under 43 percent.

Despite being potent factors alone and in combination, money and incumbency are not the only factors affecting political races. Elections occur in an electoral context that includes both contemporary national partisan trends and the partisan makeup of the state. Or, put differently, some years and some states are simply more competitive than others. We have already noted, for example, that incumbent governors were more vulnerable in the early 1990s during a period of economic recession than during the latter half of the 1990s during a period of relative economic prosperity. Likewise, the average Democratic share of the two-party vote in gubernatorial elections has declined from a high in 1982 of 55 percent to a low in 1998 of 46 percent.

If elections vary in their competitiveness over time, they also vary over space, or, in this case, across the states. In 1998, for example, the closest gubernatorial election was in Colorado, where Republican Bill Owens edged out Democrat Gail Schoettler by less than one percent of the vote, or just 8,297 votes out of more than 1.3 million votes cast. Like most competitive elections, this was an open-seat election without gaping disparities in terms of candidate campaign finance. The victorious Republican spent just under $1.5 million (in real 1992 dollars), while his Democratic opponent spent just over $1 million. In contrast, in 1994 in Colorado, incumbent Governor Roy Romer beat his Republican opponent by sixteen points despite being significantly outspent. The Republican challenger in the race spent nearly $5.4 million, while Romer spent just under $2.6 million.

The least competitive gubernatorial election in 1998 was decided by a 73–23 percent split in Kansas. The 1998 Kansas race featured Republican incumbent Bill Graves running in a heavily Republican state. Campaign spending in the race was every bit as lopsided, with the incumbent spending nearly $2.3 million and his Democratic opposition spending only $121,752.

Over the entire twenty-year period (1978–98), New Mexico was the most competitive state in terms of the average margin of victory for the winning candidate (see table 5.2). On average, the winning candidate in gubernatorial elections in New Mexico won with a seven-point margin of victory, or slightly less than a 54–46 split of the two-party vote. Only one of the six elections, however, was decided by less than five points, and none were decided by greater than ten points. Likewise, in Virginia, one highly competitive race—the 1989 election of Douglas Wilder—is paired with a couple of marginal races (where the margin of victory is ten points or less) and a couple of races decided by thirteen- and seventeen-point margins, respectively. Surprisingly, Indiana, a state that has not gone Democratic at the presidential level since 1964, makes the list as one of the most competitive states in gubernatorial elections. As of 2004, Democrats will have controlled the governor's mansion in this "Republican" state for sixteen consecutive years. In contrast, Hawaii makes the list of competitive states despite the fact that Democrats have won every gubernatorial election since 1978. Republicans, however, have clearly made gains. In the 1998 election, Republicans lost by less than six thousand votes.

Delaware ranks as the least competitive state, where from 1988 to 1996 the winning candidates bested their opponents by margins of forty-two, thirty-two,

**Table 5.2** Most Competitive and Least Competitive States in Gubernatorial Elections, 1978–98.

| State | Average Margin of Victory |
|---|---|
| *Most Competitive* | |
| New Mexico | 7.1 |
| Virginia | 9.6 |
| Texas | 10.7 |
| Hawaii | 10.7 |
| Indiana | 11.3 |
| *Least Competitive* | |
| Delaware | 31.2 |
| Rhode Island | 27.2 |
| Maryland | 27.1 |
| Georgia | 24.8 |
| Montana | 24.6 |

and forty points, respectively. But even though elections in Delaware have not been terribly competitive, there has been partisan turnover. The 1988 election featured popular Republican incumbent Mike Castle, who outspent his opponent by a 17–1 margin. Confronted with term limits in 1992, Castle ran for Congress and was replaced by Democrat Thomas Carper, who won the open-seat election with 65 percent of the two-party vote. Carper won despite relatively equal campaign spending by the candidates. His Republican opponent spent nearly $1.3 million, just shy of the nearly $1.4 million Carper spent. When he ran for reelection in 1996, Carper spent less than half of his 1992 total ($578,528) against an underfunded Republican opponent who spent just $177,659. In the 2000 elections, Democrats maintained their hold on the governor's mansion and the state maintained its streak of relatively uncompetitive gubernatorial elections as Lieutenant Governor Ruth Ann Minner won the election with 60 percent of the two-party vote.

Like Delaware, Rhode Island has experienced considerable partisan turnover, but it has also had a tradition of uncompetitive elections. Of the ten elections held from 1978 to 1998, Democrats have won six gubernatorial elections, while Republicans have won four. In these elections, the winner has won, on average, by a twenty-seven-point margin. In contrast, all six gubernatorial elections in Maryland have gone to the Democratic Party, and generally by large margins. The one exception came amidst the Republican tidal wave of 1994, during which Republican Ellen Sauerberry came within six thousand votes of defeating Democrat Paris Glendening. In the 1994 election, Sauerberry spent just under $2 million, while her opponent spent approximately three times as much (nearly $6 million). In a 1998 rematch, Sauerberry outspent her opponent by a nearly 2–1 margin, but lost the election by a twelve-point margin.

## ELECTORAL COMPETITION AND CAMPAIGN FINANCE LAWS

As the anecdotal evidence illustrates, gubernatorial elections are a function of the partisan composition of the state, the prevailing partisan tides within a given election year, campaign spending, and incumbency (though not necessarily in this order). Within this electoral context, campaign spending is important, but is not itself the sole determinant of election outcomes. It is the recognition of the importance of spending as an influence on competition that has led reformers (and their critics) to believe that altering the flow of money into campaigns would also alter the level of competition in a given state.

But the fact that money operates as one of a number of factors determining election outcomes suggests that the effects of campaign finance laws may be less direct, and perhaps less predictable, than the campaign finance rhetoric of reformers and reform critics would lead us to believe. With respect to electoral competition, the effects of campaign finance laws are most likely indirect, meaning that reform first influences the flow of money into campaigns, and then this altered stream of cash impacts the level of competition. Based on the analyses presented in chapter 4, we know that campaign finance regulations have significant effects only on total candidate campaign spending and spending differences. So the effects of reforms, if any, on competition likely result from limits on campaign spending impacting electoral outcomes.

Campaign finance laws may also have more general effects on electoral competitiveness. For example, provisions for public financing may create an expectation that gubernatorial elections will be competitive. This expectation then becomes a sort of self-fulfilling prophecy as more experienced candidates opt to run, and then compete, at raising money and attracting votes. Party-based public financing provisions were adopted with the idea of creating a more competitive party system. While the effect on competition is intended to be more diffuse than our relatively narrow focus on gubernatorial elections, subsidizing state parties should free up monies for gubernatorial candidates. As a result, one would expect that party-based public funding mechanisms should serve to increase electoral competition.

In addition, different types of reform (public financing, contribution limits, and spending limits) are likely to have different, often unexpected, effects on gubernatorial elections. Certainly, the rhetoric surrounding issues of campaign finance regulation suggest starkly different expectations regarding the electoral effects of reform. Reformers generally defend public financing provisions as a mechanism for increasing electoral competition by equalizing the fundraising process. Meanwhile, critics of reform attack campaign spending limits, saying they limit competition by unnecessarily handicapping nonincumbent candidates (particularly challengers) who most benefit from increases in campaign spending.

Expectations regarding contribution limits are less easily defined. Initially, reformers argued that contribution limits would democratize the fundraising process, thus reducing the influence of wealthy contributors and indirectly spurring electoral competition. As noted in chapter 2, the concern over the potentially distorting influence of wealthy contributors drove much of the post–Watergate reform activity. Many, though certainly not all, reformers now believe that contribution limits are often overly restrictive, consequently increasing the time and effort needed to raise money, thereby indirectly hindering competition.

Rhetoric aside, the question of whether campaign finance regulations diminish or enhance electoral competition is ultimately an empirical one. Is electoral competition statistically different in states with and without public financing? Do relatively restrictive spending limits enhance or diminish electoral competition? Are states with more restrictive contribution limits more or less competitive?

To answer these questions we examine both the direct and indirect effects of campaign finance regulations on electoral competition. Examining the direct effects is the easier task because we can simply examine the impact of campaign finance regulations on competition within the context of a statistical model. For present purposes, our measure of competition is the margin of victory for the winning candidate, irrespective of party or incumbency. In chapter 6, we examine the partisan implications of reform, as well as the implications in races in which incumbents are seeking reelection.

As noted earlier, competition is driven by campaign spending (measured on a per voting age citizen basis in real dollars), incumbency, the underlying partisan divisions within a state, and prevailing partisan tides within a given election year. In table 5.3, we have also included interaction between candidate spending and incumbency, which account for the difference in the marginal return on spending by incumbent and nonincumbent candidates.[5]

As table 5.3 illustrates, while state partisanship helps set the stage, incumbency and money play the critical roles in determining the competitiveness of gubernatorial elections. The unstandardized regression coefficient of .25 for the competition variable indicates that those states with more balanced partisan divisions also have more competitive gubernatorial elections, while states with greater partisan imbalances are less competitive.

When incumbents seek reelection, the expected margin of victory increases by approximately ten points, regardless of whether the incumbent is a Democrat or a Republican. In other words, in the average open-seat race, the winning

**Table 5.3** OLS Regressions of Margin of Victory on State Campaign Finance Regulations, 1978–98

| Variable | Margin of Victory (Absolute Value) |
|---|---|
| Democratic Spending per Voting Age Citizen | 1.68 (.98) |
| Republican Spending per Voting Age Citizen | –4.68 (1.18)** |
| Democratic Incumbent | 10.46 (2.28)** |
| Republican Incumbent | 10.09 (3.40)** |
| Democratic Spending X Democratic Incumbent | –3.09 (1.19)** |
| Republican Spending X Republican Incumbent | –.03 (2.09) |
| Partisanship/Competition | .25 (.06)* |
| Spending Limits | .68 (3.55) |
| Spending Limits per Voting Age Citizen | –1.38 (3.25) |
| Contribution Limits | –.23 (.37) |
| Public Financing to Parties | –2.07 (1.77) |
| Constant | 8.83 (2.67)** |
| R-squared | .30 |

Note: For the purposes of presentation, year variables are not included in the table. The full regression estimates are available upon request from the authors. Panel-corrected standard errors are in parentheses.* $p < .05$; ** $p < .01$.

candidate wins with a 54–46 split in the two-party vote. When an incumbent seeks reelection, this increases to a difference of 59–41.

Campaign spending also plays an important role in producing competitive elections, though unlike incumbency, the effects depend on the candidate's party. For example, for each additional dollar spent by a Republican nonincumbent candidate, the margin of victory declines by approximately 4.7 points. Democratic nonincumbent spending, on the other hand, is not associated with more competitive elections, while Democratic incumbent spending is, presumably, because Democratic incumbents are vulnerable to a Republican challenge. Rather than assuming that Republican spending is an effective stimulus of electoral competition, we believe this finding reflects the broader electoral context. In the period under study, Republicans made consistent gains in terms of controlling state governorships, particularly in the South.

In terms of the campaign finance regulations, we find no significant direct effects on electoral competition. This finding does not mean, however, that reform has no effect, but rather that the effects manifest themselves through changes in candidate campaign spending. Recall that in chapter 4 we delineated the impact of campaign finance regulations on candidate campaign spending. Using these estimates, we can now estimate the indirect effects of these regulations on gubernatorial competition by multiplying the change in candidate campaign spending induced by a state campaign finance regulation by the effect of campaign spending on gubernatorial competition. [6] Because we found no evidence of any direct effects of party-based public funding on candidate campaign spending, and because the effects of contribution limits were limited to incumbent and total spending, we have confined the discussion of indirect effects to candidate-based public financing with spending limits.

As was noted in chapter 4, the effect of candidate-based public financing on candidate campaign spending depends very much on the level of the limit and the source of the spending. For example, in a state with public financing and spending limits set at $1.00 per voting age citizen, and assuming an open-seat election, we would expect Republican spending to increase by $0.11 per voting age citizen, while Democratic spending would be expected to increase by $0.44. In contrast, in a state with limits set at $0.50 per citizen, Republican spending would be expected to decrease by $0.07 per citizen, while Democratic spending would be expected to increase by $0.02 per citizen. The effects of these changes in spending on electoral competition are presented in figure 5.3, first under the assumption of an open-seat election, and second under the assumption of a Democratic incumbent seeking reelection. Because Republican incumbent spending was not associated with more competitive gubernatorial elections (in an absolute sense), the pattern for Republican incumbents should be similar to the pattern for open-seat elections (and consequently was left out of figure 5.3).

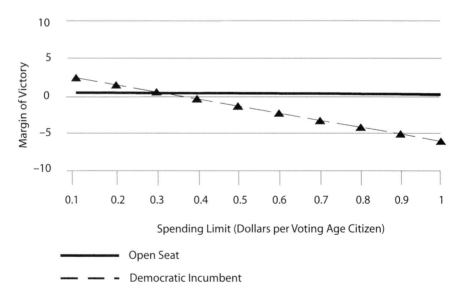

**Figure 5.3** Predicted Effects of Candidate-Based Public Financing and Spending Limits on the Margin of Victory in Gubernatorial Elections, 1978–98

As can be seen in figure 5.3, the effects of candidate-based public financing on gubernatorial competition depend very much on the restrictiveness of the associated spending limits. In open-seat elections, the effects are largely inconsequential. While we would expect slightly less competitive elections, the indirect effects range from less than a half percent increase with a $.10 per voting age citizen spending limit to just more than a fifth of a percent increase with a $1.00 per voting age citizen limit. With a Democratic incumbent running for reelection, the effects are more substantial, ranging from an increase in the margin of victory of nearly 2.5 percent with the limit set at $.10 per voting age citizen, to a 6 percent decrease in the margin with the limit set at $1.00. Overall, a combination of candidate-based public financing and spending limits has little effect on open-seat elections and in elections where Republican incumbents seek reelection, but has a much more substantial effect on Democratic incumbents. The effects are contingent upon the level of any associated spending limits, but under most scenarios (and the scenarios that most closely approximate state spending limits), the margin of victory declines. While the analysis does not speak specifically to this question, declining margins of victory presumably work to the disadvantage of the incumbent.

## CONCLUSIONS

Underlying partisan divisions within a state set the stage for electoral competition. But if these partisan divisions determine what is possible, the drama of any given election is played out largely by the intersection of money and incumbency. From the standpoint of campaign finance reform, this intersection means that election laws that influence the flow of money into gubernatorial elections may also alter the competitive balance within a state. Because campaign finance regulations are only one of several factors that influence candidate campaign spending, and because campaign spending is itself only one of several factors that influence electoral competition, the effects of changes in campaign finance laws on electoral competition are unlikely to be as clearcut as either reformers or their supporters claim.

For one, while money is important in gubernatorial elections, incumbency remains a powerful, often insurmountable, force. Also, as demonstrated in chapter 4, the effect of campaign finance laws on the flow of money into election campaigns is often different from what supporters and opponents claim. As a result, rhetoric that campaign finance reform would either greatly diminish or greatly facilitate electoral competition is often overblown. First, as we have documented, the electoral effects of campaign finance regulations depend very much on the nature of the regulations in place. Put simply, public financing with spending limits set at $.50 per voter will have a different effect than public financing with spending limits set at $1.00 per voter. Second, the effects also depend on both candidate type (incumbent v. challenger) and partisanship (Democrat v. Republican). Specifically, we find substantial effects for those elections where a Democratic incumbent is running for reelection, but not in races without an incumbent or where a Republican incumbent is seeking reelection. In races involving Democratic incumbents, candidate-based public financing combined with spending limits does appear to close the electoral margin—at least as long as any associated spending limits are not overly restrictive.

Because we have measured competition in terms of the margin of victory for the winning candidate irrespective of partisanship and incumbency, however, we cannot say that campaign finance regulations advantage Democrats over Republicans or incumbents over challengers. Deciphering the effects of campaign finance regulations on partisan and incumbent success in gubernatorial elections is the task we turn to in chapter 6.

# 6

## State Campaign Finance and Electoral Outcomes

Even where none is intended, bias is an inevitable part of our political and legal systems. The law may be blind but it is rarely neutral. Changing existing laws alters the nature of the bias, perhaps minimizing it but never eliminating it completely. Which is another way of saying that rules matter, and that they have consequences—both in terms of how the game is played and who wins and who loses. Yet, because of the uncertainty of human nature, these consequences may be much different from what was intended or expected. The law of unintended consequences certainly holds true in the area of campaign finance regulation, where a suspicious, wary eye is cast upon any regulation that falls under the rubric of electoral reform. In previous chapters, we discussed the consequences of campaign finance regulations with respect to candidate campaign spending and electoral competition. In this chapter, we focus even more narrowly on what is perhaps the most pressing issue of consequence: who wins and who loses.

### THE INCUMBENCY ADVANTAGE AND CAMPAIGN FINANCE REGULATIONS

In debates over campaign finance reform, much is said about which candidates are likely to reap the electoral benefits of campaign finance regulations, but with little direct evidence. Earlier we discussed the reasons why direct evidence is so sparse, so we need not repeat the arguments here. We do, however, want to briefly reiterate some of the expected effects of campaign finance regulations on electoral outcomes based on both reformist and opposition rhetoric.

For advocates of campaign finance reform, public financing serves as an electoral Robin Hood, redistributing resources to candidates in greatest need, thus enhancing their efforts to win elected office. As was noted in the introduction, Jesse Ventura represents the hope of campaign finance reform: a candidate unable to compete in the traditional campaign finance market who uses public financing to first become competitive and then to win the competition. Contribution limits serve a similar purpose: democratizing campaign fundraising by limiting the power of a few wealthy contributors to control election outcomes. Both public financing and contribution limits suggest that nonincumbent candidates should benefit in states that do more to regulate gubernatorial campaigns in the form of public financing provisions (with spending limits) and contribution limits.

Not surprisingly, critics of campaign finance regulation view limits differently than do supporters. Opponents see spending limits as not only unconstitutional but also as an ill-advised and unnecessary restraint on those challengers best positioned to defeat a sitting incumbent. Nonincumbent candidates compete against the power of incumbency with money, first by buying name recognition to establish viability and then by communicating the messages needed to win votes. In addition, some opponents of reform think contribution limits also hurt nonincumbents while helping incumbents. They reason that contribution limits increase the already herculean task of campaign fundraising by requiring candidates to raise money from a longer list of potential contributors and thus unintentionally further protect those already in power who have established name recognition and contributor lists. Following Watergate, wealthy contributors were seen as a root cause of a corrupted political process. Reforms aimed at diminishing their influence by limiting the size of political contributions also increased the time and energy necessary to raise the type of money needed to be a serious candidate in contemporary American politics. The burden is most severe for those candidates on the outside of power looking in. Both arguments suggest a clear empirical expectation; that is, nonincumbent gubernatorial candidates should find electoral victory more elusive in states that do more to regulate gubernatorial campaigns through public financing, spending limits, and contribution limits.

A cursory glance at the various measures of reform and the incumbent share of the vote suggests that neither view may be realized in actual gubernatorial campaigns, particularly if one confines his or her attention to the direct effects of campaign finance regulations on electoral outcomes. As can be seen in table 6.1, the differences across elections with a specific campaign finance regulation in place versus those without such a provision are quite small. For example, in elections with candidate-based public financing, incumbents averaged roughly 57 percent of the vote. In elections without candidate-based public financing provisions, incumbents averaged just under 59 percent of the vote. While the difference supports reformist arguments, it is too small to conclude with any confidence that incumbents are more vulnerable in states with public financing.

**Table 6.1** Average Incumbent Share of the Vote in Gubernatorial Elections and the Absence or Presence of Campaign Finance Regulations, 1978–98

| | Mean Incumbent Vote | |
|---|---|---|
| **Campaign Finance Regulation** | **Absence of Regulation** | **Presence of Regulation** |
| Corporation Contribution Limits | 58.67 | 58.60 |
| Union Contribution Limits | 59.04 | 58.40 |
| Individual Contribution Limits | 58.35 | 58.81 |
| PACS Contribution Limits | 59.07 | 58.14 |
| Family Member Contribution Limits | 58.58 | 58.68 |
| Candidate Contribution Limits | 58.52 | 59.50 |
| Public Financing to Parties | 58.48 | 59.22 |
| Public Financing to Candidates | 58.97 | 57.01 |

Note: None of these differences are statistically significant at the .05 level.

To better assess the impact of campaign finance regulations on the incumbent vote, we used a regression model which includes controls for candidate campaign spending, partisanship, national trends, and underlying patterns of electoral competition.[1] As can be seen in table 6.2, electoral outcomes in elections involving incumbents are largely driven by challenger campaign spending and the overall level of competition within the state. In this respect, the incumbent percentage of the vote declines roughly 5 percent for each additional dollar per voting age citizen spent by the challenger. Incumbent spending does not have a similar effect, presumably because incumbents are usually well known and have a record (good or bad) on which to run.[2]

**Table 6.2** Regressions of Incumbent Percentage of the Vote on State Campaign Finance Regulations, 1978–98

| Variable | Incumbent Percentage of the Vote |
|---|---|
| Incumbent Spending per Voting Age Citizen | .34 (.55) |
| Challenger Spending per Voting Age Citizen | -5.02 (1.03)** |
| Democratic Incumbent | 1.76 (1.50) |
| Electoral Overall Competition | .12 (.06)* |
| Public Financing to Candidates | -4.22 (2.21)* |
| Spending Limits per Voting Age Citizen | .53 (2.26) |
| Contribution Limits | -.02 (.39) |
| Public Financing to Parties | 1.49 (1.74) |
| Constant | 57.67 (2.42)** |
| R-squared | .33 |

Note: For the purposes of presentation, year variables are not included in the table. The full regression estimates are available upon request from the authors. Standard errors are in parentheses. $^* p < .05$; $^{**} p < .01$.

In addition to candidate spending and electoral competition, incumbent success rates are associated with candidate-based public financing provisions. According to the estimates in table 6.2, gubernatorial challengers run over four points stronger in states with public financing than in states without such provisions. While critics of reform might argue that the results may be misleading to a certain degree (saying, for example, that not all candidates accept public financing or that the finding may reflect other differences between states with and without public financing provisions), arguments that public financing laws protect incumbents appear to be, at best, overstated. On average, incumbents are more, rather than less, vulnerable in states with public financing provisions. The availability of public funding may either encourage stronger challengers to run against an incumbent or it may give potential challengers a way to boost their credibility that is not available to candidates running in states without public funding provisions. The boost provided by public funding may help candidates overcome the Catch-22 confronting them as they challenge incumbents; that is, how to attract supporters, financial and otherwise, in order to run a serious campaign when individuals are hesitant to give their support because they are not sure the candidate has enough support to run a serious campaign. The direct benefits public financing provides to gubernatorial challengers are not, however, mitigated by any corresponding spending limits. By this we mean that, after controlling for any associated changes in candidate campaign spending, challengers are no less successful in states with relatively restrictive spending limits than in states with more generous limits.

Contribution limits and party-based public financing also appear to be unrelated to the incumbent percentage of the vote. As a result, incumbents are no more, nor any less, vulnerable in states which engage in greater regulation of campaign contributions or which provide public subsidies to state political parties.

## INDIRECT EFFECTS OF CAMPAIGN FINANCE REGULATIONS ON INCUMBENTS AND CHALLENGERS

In addition to direct effects, campaign finance regulations may have indirect effects caused by changes in candidate campaign spending. These indirect effects, however, are likely to be fairly marginal. Recall that in chapter 4 we found no evidence to indicate that challenger spending was significantly affected by any of the reform provisions included in our analysis (candidate-based public financing, party-based financing, spending limits, or contribution limits). Because challenger spending is most closely associated with the incumbent share of the vote, and because it is relatively immune to the effects of campaign finance regulations, the changes induced in candidate campaign spending by campaign finance regulations should have only minor effects on the incumbent share of the vote.

While we did find that incumbent spending was affected by both contribution limits and a combination of candidate-based public financing and spending limits, we failed to find significant effects of incumbent spending on the incumbent share of the vote.[3] The rather curious result is that reform efforts have their greatest impact on the least effective source of candidate campaign spending. Consequently, campaign finance regulations—at least as they have been realized in the U.S. states (and measured in this analysis)—have only marginal indirect effects on incumbent success rates.

For example, if we limited spending to only $.10 per voting age citizen (while also providing public funding), incumbent spending would be expected to decline by approximately $.43 per voting age citizen, while challenger spending would be expected to decline by $.14.[4] As a result of these changes, the incumbent percentage of the vote would be expected to increase by just over a half of one percent. Alternatively, if a state limited spending to $1.00 per voting age citizen (with candidate-based public financing), incumbent spending would be expected to increase by $.56 per voting age citizen, while challenger spending would be expected to increase by $.09. Under this scenario, the incumbent percentage of the vote would be expected to decrease by just over a quarter of a percent.

As with public financing, contribution limits have a marginal impact on the incumbent percentage of the vote. Even in a state that restricts each type of contribution, the impact on the incumbent vote would be expected to be less than a half of one percent. Put simply, contribution limits do not make incumbents any more, or any less, vulnerable.

Overall, we find no evidence that campaign finance regulations protect incumbents or hurt challengers. If anything, public financing provisions make incumbents more vulnerable, and the supposed adverse effects on challengers are marginal. Thus, while campaign finance reform is no panacea, its adverse effects are, at best, "overstated."

## THE PARTISAN CONSEQUENCES OF CAMPAIGN FINANCE REGULATIONS

From the effects on incumbents and challengers, debates over campaign finance regulations inevitably lead to expectations regarding reform's partisan consequences. Parties and candidates are, of course, circumspect about how electoral self-interest might shape preferences on campaign finance reform and may prefer to couch support or opposition in First Amendment principles or in the language of democratic political equality. Still, if we assume that political parties are self-interested actors—that is, they are both aware of their self-interest and act accordingly—then political debates over campaign finance reform would suggest that Democrats would benefit from more heavily regulated political campaigns, in terms of both contribution limits and public financing. Though there are differences across states and years, because Democrats tend to be less successful raising money, they would be more likely to benefit from campaign finance regulations. Democrats have consistently (though often superficially) supported reform at the national level and have generally been more support-ive than the Republicans at the state level as well.

Republicans—as members of the party advocating smaller government—have often resisted efforts aimed at regulating national and state campaign finance, presumably because they are better at raising money than their Dem-ocratic opponents. Over the last several decades, Republican Party organizations have clearly outpaced their Democratic counterparts in campaign fundraising.[5]

Differences in party fundraising efforts, however, have not always translated into differences in candidate spending. On average, Democratic candidates out-spend their Republican opposition, though the statistic is somewhat misleading. Average Democratic spending was $1.28 per voting age citizen, while average Republican spending was $1.19. Despite the higher average Democratic spend-ing, Republican gubernatorial candidates outspent their Democratic opponents in 53 percent of the gubernatorial races from 1978 to 1998. So, in the typical guber-natorial race, the Republican candidate outspends the Democratic candidate.

Whether spending patterns are affected by campaign finance regulations is not immediately clear. They do, however, suggest that expectations regarding the partisan consequences of campaign finance reform may be more muddled than the rhetoric of reform might indicate. Political scientist Ruth Jones, for example, found in a 1981 study that the minority party generally benefits from public financing provisions.[6] For most of the period under study, then, it may be Repub-licans rather than Democrats who benefit from public financing provisions.

To get a first glimpse of the partisan consequences of campaign finance reg-ulations, we examine the average Democratic share of the vote in states with and without various campaign finance provisions (see table 6.3). While most of the differences are not large and fail to reach the level of statistical significance, in six of eight categories the average Democratic vote was lower in states with those particular types of campaign finance provisions. The only statistically significant difference involves states that limit union contributions. In these states, Demo-cratic gubernatorial candidates run, on average, three points behind their Republican opposition. Because most states that restrict union contributions also restrict corporate contributions, there is a similar difference in states with and without corporate contribution limits. Overall, and contrary to conven-tional wisdom, Democratic gubernatorial candidates fare worse in states which do more to regulate campaign activity.

A fuller account of the partisan consequences of campaign finance reform requires accounting for differences across states in terms of candidate campaign

**Table 6.3** Average Democratic Share of the Vote in Gubernatorial Elections and the Absence or Presence of Campaign Finance Regulations, 1978–98

| | Mean Democratic Vote | |
|---|---|---|
| Campaign Finance Regulation | Absence of Regulation | Presence of Regulation |
| Corporation Contribution Limits | 53.11 | 50.58 |
| Union Contribution Limits* | 53.42 | 50.32 |
| Individual Contribution Limits | 52.01 | 51.10 |
| PACS Contribution Limits | 51.81 | 51.09 |
| Family Member Contribution Limits | 51.86 | 50.88 |
| Candidate Contribution Limits | 51.46 | 51.67 |
| Public Financing to Parties | 51.74 | 50.46 |
| Public Financing to Candidates | 51.46 | 51.56 |

Note: * $p < .05$.

spending, electoral competition, incumbency, and national partisan tides.[7] We do so using a regression model that takes into account the pooled time series nature of the data. As can be seen in table 6.4, the Democratic percentage of the vote is largely a function of candidate campaign spending, incumbency, and the underlying partisan divisions within the state. For candidates in open-seat races, the effect of campaign spending is roughly equivalent, with both Democrats and Republicans yielding about three to three and a half percent of the vote for each additional dollar per voting age citizen spent. Republican incumbents, however, have a clear advantage over their Democratic counterparts. Republican incumbents receive an additional two percent of the vote for each additional dollar spent, while spending by Democratic incumbents actually has an adverse (though inconsequential) impact on their share of the vote.

Notably, however, the value of Democratic incumbency, when controlling for campaign spending, is considerably higher than the value of Republican incumbency. On average, Democratic incumbents run 12 percent better than Democratic nonincumbents, while Republican incumbents run just 7.5 points ahead of Republican nonincumbents. Taken in the context of the findings on campaign spending, this means that Democratic incumbents start with a larger base advantage, but that their campaign spending is a relatively ineffectual means for padding that advantage. Republican incumbents, on the other hand, start with a smaller advantage, but find some salvation through additional campaign spending.

Consistent with our comparisons of mean differences in the Democratic vote, each of our measures of campaign finance regulations exerts a negative (though statistically insignificant) effect on the Democratic vote. In other words, controlling for the other factors included in the model, there are no systematic differences in the Democratic percentage of the vote in states that have these

**Table 6.4** Regression of the Democratic Vote on State Campaign Finance Regulations, 1978–98

| Variable | Democratic Percentage of the Vote |
|---|---|
| Democratic Spending per Voting Age Citizen | ︱3.50 (.76)** |
| Republican Spending per Voting Age Citizen | −3.27 (.78)** |
| Democratic Incumbent | 12.33 (1.54)** |
| Republican Incumbent | −7.56 (2.42)** |
| Democratic Spending X Democratic Incumbent | −3.61 (.82)** |
| Republican Spending X Republican Incumbent | 1.06 (1.63) |
| Partisanship | .23 (.05)** |
| Public Financing to Candidates | −.68 (1.76) |
| Spending Limits per Voting Age Citizen | −1.82 (1.41) |
| Contribution Limits | −.26 (.26) |
| Public Financing to Parties | −1.13 (1.10) |
| Constant | 38.83 (3.03)** |
| R-square *explained variance* | .52 |

Note: For the purposes of presentation, year variables are not included in the table. The full regression estimates are available upon request from the authors. Standard errors are in parentheses.* $p < .05$; ** $p < .01$.

campaign finance provisions versus those states without such regulations. Given that campaign finance regulations, particularly candidate-based public financing provisions, exert a significant effect on both Republican and Democratic campaign spending, these indirect effects are at least potentially more substantial. Because these provisions impact both Democratic and Republican campaign spending, however, the effect on Republican candidates may be minimized by a similar effect on Democratic candidates.

Recall from chapter 4 that the effect of candidate-based public financing on Democratic and Republican campaign spending is contingent upon the level of any associated spending limits. Under some scenarios, candidate spending declines, while under a different set of limits candidate spending increases. Moreover, because Republican and Democratic spending do not decline or increase at the same rate, the partisan consequences of reform depend on the type of reform scenario in question as well as candidate type (incumbent v. nonincumbent) and partisanship. Figure 6.1 presents these relationships graphically under various reform scenarios ranging from a $.10 to a $1.00 per voting age citizen limit.

With an open-seat election and at a $.10 per voter spending limit, the Democratic percentage of the vote would be expected to decrease by less than a half of a percent. In other words, at least in open-seat elections, highly restrictive limits work to the disadvantage of the Democratic candidate, though the effect is fairly marginal. With a $1.00 per voting age citizen limit, the advantage would shift to the Democratic candidate. Under this scenario, the Democratic

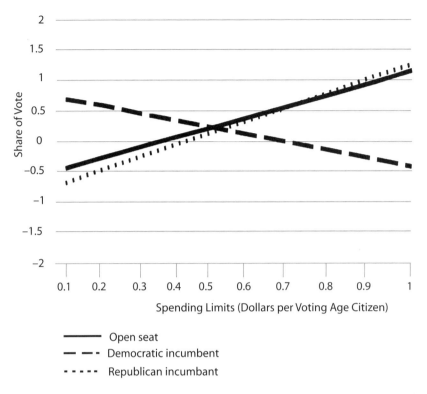

**Figure 6.1** Predicted Effects of Candidate-based Public Financing and Spending Limits on the Democratic Share of the Vote

vote would be expected to increase by roughly one percent. The relationship is almost identical when there is a Republican incumbent running for reelection, but is markedly different when the incumbent is a Democrat. With a Democratic incumbent running, more restrictive limits work to the incumbent's advantage, while less restrictive limits work to his or her disadvantage. At a $.10 per voting age citizen limit, the Democratic vote would be expected to increase by seven-tenths of one percent. At the other end of the chart, however, the Democratic percentage of the vote would be expected to decrease by roughly one-third of one percent when limits are set at $1.00 per voting age citizen.

On balance, Democratic nonincumbents appear to get the best deal out of campaign finance regulations. First, Democratic spending increases more than Republican spending under all but the most restrictive candidate-based public financing scenarios; and second, Democratic spending has a significant effect on the partisan vote (roughly equivalent to that of Republican spending). As such, Democrats running in open-seat elections and those running against

Republican incumbents appear to be the prime beneficiaries of campaign finance regulations. In this respect, partisan rhetoric does appear to reflect electoral realities. Yet, it is also worth noting that even under the best case scenarios (from a Democratic perspective), the effect is unlikely to be much more than a percent of the partisan vote.

## CONCLUSIONS

Who wins and who loses when a state adopts campaign finance regulations? The strength of the resistance and the commitment to reform seem to suggest the consequences of regulations are considerable. Our analysis, however, suggests consequences are much smaller in scale. The most substantial effect is the four-point difference in the incumbent vote share in states with candidate-based public financing provisions. In these states, incumbents do appear to be more electorally vulnerable—even after controlling for candidate campaign spending and the base level of competition within the state. While we cannot entirely rule out the possibility that the relationship is caused more by the types of states with candidate-based public financing provisions in place than by the enactment of reform itself, it does call into question claims that reform is incumbency protection.

In terms of the indirect effects of reform that occur through changes in candidate campaign spending, we found little evidence of any systematic biases (either positive or negative) on incumbents seeking reelection. According to our results, campaign finance regulations have their most pronounced effects on incumbent campaign spending, but because incumbent spending does not exert a significant impact on the incumbent's share of the vote, the effect of these changes has little impact on electoral outcomes. Notably, had we found that incumbent spending exerted an effect on the incumbent share of the vote similar in size to that of challenger spending, our conclusions would have been even more supportive of reformist arguments.[8]

The partisan consequences of reform were even less substantial. On balance, Democratic nonincumbents benefit more than Republicans or Democratic incumbents, but even here the effects are fairly small and would be of consequence only in the most competitive elections. Overall, Democratic candidates have a slight advantage, but it is unlikely that many observers would notice the advantage.

# CHAPTER 7

## State Campaign Finance and Voter Turnout

On this much there is widespread agreement: by definition, democracy should give citizens the opportunity to participate in the policy-making process. However, the nature of the opportunity and the role of the government in assuring that opportunity is realized, the avenues of participation and the meaningfulness of participation, as well as the very meaning of the "consent of the governed," remain in dispute.

For James Madison, the public voice needed to be heavily filtered. Through the aristocratic Senate, the indirect election of the President by the Electoral College, the appointment of unelected keepers of the law on the Supreme Court, and the intricate system of checks and balances, he thought the red hot passion of the public that would enter the House of Representatives full of majoritarian impulse would leave ice cold as a reasoned and incremental response cooled the burning issues of the day. But if this is the reality of Madisonian democracy, we believe in something very different. The Jeffersonian ideal that all men are created equal, Jacksonian democracy in which the public may be vulgar and crass but it is their government, and the Populist, the Progressive, and Civil Rights movements have melded the Madisonian philosophy closer in line with democratic ideals. Seen in this light, the history of the American political system has, at least in part, been a history of the reconciliation of the democratic creed with the reality of a Madisonian republic.

The link between philosophies is a belief (well supported by evidence) that laws and political institutions can structure and filter political participation, either to enhance or diminish its influence. Laws closely related to the act of voting—particularly voter registration laws—have a clear impact on voter turnout, though easing registration requirements (e.g., motor voter laws) has had a more limited impact on voter turnout than one might suspect.[1] Likewise, the timing of elections also influences voter participation. For example, turnout in gubernatorial elections is, on average, ten to fifteen points higher during presidential as opposed to off-year elections. Ironically, decisions to limit the influence of national factors in state elections may have had the unintended consequence of limiting the level of public participation in collective decisions on state executive leadership.[2]

For present purposes, we ask a related but different question; that is, do campaign finance laws hinder or facilitate citizen participation? Answers to the question from political activists highlight fundamentally different assumptions about the nature of participation in a democratic polity. According to critics of campaign finance reform, money is not just a means to participation, it is itself a mode of participation. For those lacking the time or the interest to participate through other avenues, writing a check can successfully communicate a political preference while offsetting the participation of those with the time and energy to participate more directly. Seen in this light, money is just one resource of many that can influence political debate and any pursuant outcomes.

Not surprisingly, given this view, critics of reform contend that contribution and spending limits are themselves restrictions on individual participation. More interesting from our perspective is the possibility that campaign finance laws limit voter participation by either (1) reducing the amount of money available to be spent on voter mobilization efforts or (2) reducing the amount of money available for direct communication with voters (via advertisements or direct mail) and thus reducing information and interest in the campaign which in turn reduces voter turnout.

For supporters of reform, checkbook participation serves not as a mode of participation, but either as an exercise in corruption, and contaminant of democratic processes, or as an amplification of participation for those with the resources to vote their pocketbook. Either way, the result is a declining faith not only in public officials but also in political institutions. In the language of reform, this declining civic faith translates into fewer votes and fewer voters.

But declining faith is not the only drag on electoral participation. Money may mobilize and inform voters, but much depends on the messages that are conveyed. While the jury is still out on the causal link between negative campaigns and voter turnout, there is at least some suggestive evidence that negativity depresses voter participation.[3] And though campaign spending may inform voters, thus stimulating their interest in the campaign, it may also leave them scratching their heads, particularly where candidates seek the median voter (assuming a normal distribution of opinion) by remaining intentionally ambiguous or moderating their opinions on divisive issues.[4]

Any potential mobilizing effect of campaign spending is also contingent on how, and by whom, the money is spent. At least in congressional races, much of the money spent by the candidates has little to do with actually communicating with voters.[5] But even if it were so, studies indicate that some forms of communication are, not surprisingly, more effective than others. Political scientists Alan S. Gerber and Donald P Green, for example, found that personal canvassing had a substantial impact on voter turnout, direct mail had only a slight impact, and telephone calls had no impact at all. As their study illustrates, interpersonal contact (via canvassing) has a much higher return than more impersonal efforts (direct mail and telephone calls).[6] Because the study focused on nonpartisan efforts at increasing voter turnout, it is possible that partisan efforts at mobilizing turnout have different rates of return. More specifically, the effect of partisan mobilization efforts may depend on the type of voter being contacted, as well as on other contextual factors, including the source of the spending.[7] As is the case with electoral competition, at least in congressional elections, challenger spending yields more bang for the buck in terms of voter turnout.[8]

Overall, higher spending does not necessarily translate into higher voter turnout. Much depends on what messages are being conveyed as well as how, and by whom, the money is spent. Within this context, campaign finance laws could directly impact voter turnout by either influencing the total amount of money spent or by influencing the means by which money enters the electoral process. Alternatively, campaign finance laws could indirectly influence voter turnout by increasing citizen trust in state governing institutions or perceptions of political efficacy. Before providing a fuller evaluation of the impact of campaign finance laws on voter turnout, we first consider the patterns and explanations of voter turnout in gubernatorial elections.

## PATTERNS OF TURNOUT IN GUBERNATORIAL ELECTIONS

In the average state, voter turnout for gubernatorial elections is 46 percent; but this average masks considerable variance across states and over time in voter participation rates. The largest differences occur between states with gubernatorial elections in off-years (which includes both midterms and odd-numbered years) versus those with elections in presidential election years. In off-year elections, average voter turnout is just under 43 percent.[9] In presidential election years, average voter turnout is over 58 percent. It might be tempting to attribute this difference solely to the presence of a presidential race. States with gubernatorial elections during presidential years tend to have higher voter turnout than states without gubernatorial elections in the same years. For example, in 1996, national voter turnout was 49 percent, while the average for states with gubernatorial elections was 55 percent. The pattern is similar for the four other presidential election years included in the data set, with vote turnout, on average, roughly five to ten points higher in states with gubernatorial elections.

In national elections, voter turnout has—with the exception of 1992—been steadily declining since at least the 1960s. And while, historically, states have experienced a similar decline, the decline is not very apparent over the period of this study (1978–98).[10] Looking just at midterm gubernatorial elections, in 1978, average voter turnout was 42 percent, while in 1998, voter turnout was 41 percent. Between 1978 and 1998, voter turnout in all gubernatorial elections fluctuated from just under 41 percent to just over 46 percent. If we consider a similar time frame for presidential elections (1976–96), the decline in voter turnout in national elections is not as apparent. In 1976, national voter turnout was approximately 53.5 percent. By 1996, it had declined to 49 percent, but only after a third-party induced bump to 55 percent in 1992. In the 2000 presidential election, voter turnout increased slightly to 51.2 percent—despite the most competitive election in over four decades.

The highest voter turnout in any gubernatorial election from 1978 to 1998 was a 76 percent turnout in Vermont in 1992. Surprisingly, the election itself was neither highly competitive nor highly expensive. The election did occur in a presidential election year, in which Bill Clinton carried the state by more than twenty

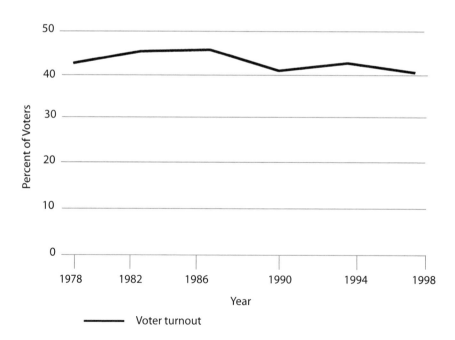

**Figure 7.1** Voter Turnout in Gubernatorial Elections, 1978–98 (Midterms Only)

points. In the 1992 gubernatorial election, Democrat Howard Dean, a former lieutenant governor who became governor when his Republican predecessor, Richard Snelling, died of a heart attack while in office, won with 75 percent of the two-party vote. Dean spent $257,706, but still outspent his Republican opponent by over a hundred thousand dollars. Over a hundred thousand more voters turned out in Vermont during the presidential election year of 1992 than in the much more competitive and more expensive open-seat election of 1990. In the 1990 election, Republican Richard Snelling won with 54 percent of the vote, just six points ahead of his Democratic opponent, but voter turn out lagged at just 49 percent. In 1994, turnout was again 49 percent, despite a much more lopsided race, won by incumbent Howard Dean with 69 percent of the vote.

The lowest voter turnout during this period of study was in Georgia in 1978, where only 19 percent of eligible voters turned out to cast a ballot on election day. (One would have thought political interest would have been greater in Georgia at the time, since the state's Jimmy Carter was at the midpoint of his presidential administration.) Incumbent Democratic Governor George Busbee easily won reelection with 81 percent of the vote. Like most low voter turnout elections, the campaign was one-sided both in terms of the margin of victory and campaign spending. Busbee outspent his opponent nearly 6–1, even though he only spent roughly $635,000 (in real 1992 dollars).

While turnout in the 1978 election was low even for a midterm election in Georgia, all five of Georgia's gubernatorial elections from 1978 to 1998 had relatively modest voter turnout. Georgia experienced its highest voter turnout in a 1990 open-seat contest in which current Georgia Senator Zell Miller rode the promise of lottery funds for education into the governor's mansion. Even in this election, defined by a major issue, with total spending just under $10 million (in real 1992 dollars), and only eight points separating Miller from his Republican opponent, only a third of the voting age population turned out to vote.

As is the case with Georgia, voter turnout is generally lowest in Southern states. In fact, if we create top five lists of states with the lowest and highest averages in voter turnout from 1978 to 1998 (see table 7.1), all five of the lowest turnout states are from the South, and none of these states hold gubernatorial elections during presidential election years. These are also states which political scientist Daniel Elazar classifies as having traditionalistic political cultures.[11] In traditionalistic cultures, government intervention (except in those cases where it is necessary to defend the status quo) is viewed with suspicion. In contrast, the highest turnout states tend to be from the West and have coinciding gubernatorial and presidential elections. They also have cultures that Elazar classifies as moralistic; that is, they place value on equality and have the view that government ought to pursue the common good. More receptive to government intervention, moralistic political cultures are also more participatory in nature. The

**Table 7.1** Highest and Lowest Average Voter Turnout by State in Gubernatorial Elections, 1978–98

| State | Average Voter Turnout |
| --- | --- |
| *Highest Turnout* | |
| Utah | 66 |
| Montana | 65 |
| North Dakota | 64 |
| Washington | 59 |
| Missouri | 59 |
| *Lowest Turnout* | |
| Kentucky | 35 |
| South Carolina | 33 |
| Tennessee | 33 |
| Texas | 31 |
| Georgia | 29 |

one exception in the top five is Missouri, which Elazar classifies as having an individualistic/traditionalistic political culture. Unlike the other states included in the top five, high voter turnout in Missouri has less to do with political culture than with Missouri's status as a battleground state in presidential elections.

Among states that hold gubernatorial elections during midterm years, the highest average turnout was in Minnesota (also classified as having a moralistic political culture), where 56 percent of voting age adults turn out in the average election. Among states that hold gubernatorial elections during presidential elections years, North Carolina and West Virginia scraped the bottom in terms of average voter turnout. In both states, average voter turnout was roughly 50 percent.

Besides the timing of the election and region of the country, voter turnout is influenced by the demographic profile of the state. From studies of individual voter participation, we know that socioeconomic status (which includes education, income, and occupational prestige) is associated with a higher probability of individual voter turnout.[12] At the aggregate level, one would suspect states with more educated and wealthier electorates to display higher levels of voter turnout. Yet, there are also reasons to suspect that state demographics may be less important than research at the individual level indicates. For one, aside from migration, state demographics are relatively stable across election years. As such, state demographics may explain aggregate propensities for statewide voter turnout, but they provide less convincing explanations of changes in turnout over time within a single state. Second, prior research has suggested that once mobilization factors are entered into the equation, the effects of state demographics are largely washed out. As Samuel Patterson and Gregory Caldeira observed in 1983, "socioeconomic characteristics, included in a fully specified model, have little to contribute independently to an explanation of voter turnout."[13] Instead, voter turnout is influenced primarily by efforts at political mobilization, including campaign spending, party organizational strength, elite ideology, and electoral competition.[14]

While the Patterson and Caldeira study did not directly address campaign finance laws, it did raise a central (though sometimes overlooked) question regarding voter turnout; that is, what policy changes might stimulate voter turnout? Patterson and Caldeira say the answer is rooted in affecting electoral competition. "Perhaps," they write, "we can make elections more competitive through immediate changes in policy, such as encouraging party organizational strength, party loyalty, a strong role for parties in the recruitment of candidates, and public funding of the political parties."

Ten years later, Steven Rosenstone and John Mark Hansen would lament the absence of politics and, by implication, policy from the study of voter turnout.[15] Where policy has been addressed in a systematic fashion, the focus has tended to be on registration requirements, with the expectation that eased registration requirements would attract voters to the polls. Writing in 1980, Raymond Wolfinger and Steven Rosenstone estimated that an additional ten million voters would turn out if registration requirements were significantly lessened.[16] Yet, even as the registration rolls have grown with the relaxing of registration requirements (such as by motor voter legislation), there has not been a significant increase in new voters.

But why should voter turnout increase? Being able to vote and wanting to vote are two separate issues, and while registration laws increase capacity, they do nothing to increase an individual's motivation to participate in the political process. Nor does an increase in the capacity serve as an incentive for parties and candidates to engage in efforts to mobilize new voters. In other words, for many potential voters, having a reason to vote is at least as important as having an opportunity, and the reason for voting relates not to registration requirements but to the types of campaigns that are being waged.

Within this context, campaign finance laws influence voter turnout only to the extent that they influence the structure of political campaigns. The most direct effect of campaign finance laws would be felt directly in the candidate's pocketbook, in his or her ability to raise and spend money. As noted earlier, critics of reform contend that any limit on candidate spending would adversely affect voter turnout, but the literature suggests otherwise. The effect of spending depends on how and by whom the money is spent. In addition, while the link between campaign spending and voter turnout has been well established, the substantive effect is often quite limited. For example, one study estimates that if spending in U.S. House races increased by $300,000, voter turnout would be expected to increase by only a half percent, or about 3,000 votes in a district with 600,000 constituents.[17]

Potentially, campaign finance laws may have direct effects on voter turnout, or perhaps more accurately, effects mediated by variables that are not included in the current analysis. For example, campaign finance laws may instill greater trust in government or increase a citizen's perception of her or his political efficacy, which in turn may translate into higher voter turnout. To estimate the effects of campaign finance laws, we constructed a regression model which includes estimates of state demographics (state per capita income, percentage of the state that is white, the size of the state, and regionalism), political mobilization (the margin of victory in the current race, state partisan competition, and campaign spending), and campaign finance laws (candidate- and party-based public financing, spending limits, and contribution limits). We also included controls for whether or not the election was an open-seat contest and for the year of the election. Including a variable for the year of the election should capture differences in presidential versus midterm years, as well as other partisan or political trends that might affect voter turnout. For ease of presentation, we left the year variables out of table 7.2.[18] In addition, because important differences exist between presidential and nonpresidential election years, we included two separate analyses: the first includes all elections and the second includes only nonpresidential election years.[19]

**Table 7.2** Regressions of State Voter Turnout on State Campaign Finance Regulations

| Variable | All Years | Off-Years |
|---|---|---|
| Democratic Spending per Voting Age Citizen | −.03 (.49) | .82 (.56) |
| Republican Spending per Voting Age Citizen | 2.10 (.60)** | 2.49 (.68)** |
| Incumbent Seeking Reelection | −.26 (.80) | −.71 (.88) |
| Percent White | .22 (.04)** | .23 (.03)** |
| Size of State | .011 (.006) | −.001 (.01) |
| South | −4.53 (1.01)** | −4.07 (1.03)** |
| Margin | −.06 (.03)* | −.09 (.04)** |
| Competition | .05 (.03) | .07 (.03)* |
| Per Capita Income | .01 (.03) | .03 (.02) |
| Contribution Limits | −.22 (.19) | −.09 (.22) |
| Spending Limits per Voting Age Citizen | −.23 (1.61) | −1.70 (2.21) |
| Public Financing to Candidates | 3.03 (1.22)** | 3.66 (1.37)** |
| Public Financing to Parties | 1.26 (.96)* | 1.91 (1.07) |
| Constant | 20.44 (3.51)** | 19.02 (3.39)** |
| R-squared | .63 | .45 |

Standard errors in parentheses
* $p < .05$; ** $p < .01$

As with Patterson and Caldeira's 1983 study, we found limited effects for the state demographic variables, but more substantial effects for political mobilization.[20] States with a higher percentage of white residents (and hence lower percentages of minorities) on average experience lower voter turnout, as do Southern states. On average, voter turnout is roughly 4 to 4.5 percent lower in Southern states.

In terms of political mobilization, both candidate spending and electoral competition influence voter turnout, but the effects are not as clear as prior research might indicate. First, as would be expected, as the margin of victory increases, voter turnout declines. But base-level competition—at least as measured by our index—appears to work in the opposite direction. That is, states that are more competitive in terms of their partisan balance tend to have lower voter turnout. While this finding may seem counterintuitive, what it really suggests is that voters are more sensitive to the contemporary election climate as opposed to the underlying partisan divisions within the state. In addition, contemporary competitiveness may be particularly important as a stimulant for political activity in less competitive states where the hard-fought election is the exception, as opposed to the rule.

Second, while campaign spending is a significant predictor of voter turnout, it is Republican as opposed to Democratic spending that appears to matter most. In this respect, each additional Republican dollar spent per voting age adult yields an estimated 2 to 2.5 percent increase in voter turnout. Democratic spending, on the other hand, yields less than a one percent increase in voter participation. Presumably, the effects are at least in part contingent upon context. Over the period of the study, Republicans have made significant inroads into Democratic control of state governor's mansions, particularly in the South. And though turnout in the South is still, on average, lower than in non-Southern states, the gap has decreased significantly over time. In 1978, voter turnout in the South averaged just 30 percent compared to 44 percent for the non-South. By 1998, average turnout in the South had actually increased to 35 percent, while turnout in non-Southern states had decreased slightly to 42 percent. The increase is undoubtedly rooted in the increased competitiveness of the Republican Party in these Southern states.[21]

Campaign finance regulations, at least public financing provisions, are also positively related to voter turnout. Although we found no evidence that contribution limits or party-based public financing significantly affect voter turnout, states which provide public financing directly to candidates have on average a 3 percent higher voter turnout than states without public financing provisions—*even after controlling for electoral competitiveness and campaign spending*. However, given the limitations of this particular analysis, we cannot say for certain what it is about the campaign finance regulations that drives this difference in aggregate voter turnout. It may be that states with more participatory cultures are also more likely to support and enact public finance provisions. Along these lines, there is some evidence to suggest that more participatory, moralistic political cultures are also less corrupt[22] and subsequently more inclined to engage in clean money reforms. It may also be that campaign finance regulations heighten perceptions of trust and efficacy, thus stimulating voter participation. But regardless of the causal mechanism, one point is indisputable: Public financing provisions are not associated with depressed voter turnout. Put simply, voters in states with public financing provisions participate at rates higher than in states without such provisions.

In addition to direct effects on voter turnout, campaign finance laws may also have indirect effects through their impact on campaign spending and electoral competition. To gauge these effects we return to our estimates in chapters 4 and 5. Recall from chapter 4 that in an open-seat election with a $.50 per citizen spending limit, Republican spending would decrease by $.05 per citizen, while Democratic spending would increase $.02. Under this scenario, the margin of victory would increase by roughly a quarter of one percent. The effect on voter turnout of these changes would, critics claim, be to reduce voter turnout but only by a tenth of one percent. If we alter the scenario by assuming a $1.00 per voting age citizen spending limit, turnout would be expected to increase by a barely perceptible 0.03 percent of eligible voters. Add an incumbent to the equation and voter turnout would be expected to decrease by 0.11 percent under the $.50 per citizen limit, and to increase by 0.15 percent assuming a $1.00 per citizen limit. In California, a decrease of 0.11 percent would amount to roughly 22,000 voters, while in Rhode Island it would equate to the loss of approximately 860 potential voters.

## CONCLUSIONS

Over the last several years, the implications of campaign finance laws on voter turnout have been hotly debated but not well understood. Prior research, which generalized from the positive correlations between voter turnout and campaign spending, has frequently been used to make the case against campaign finance reform. In this chapter, we have shown why such generalizations are based on mistaken assumptions. First, states with public financing provisions have higher voter turnout, on average, than states without such provisions. While this finding may reflect more on the type of states likely to have such provisions in the first place, it still calls into question a basic criticism of reform. States that have public financing provisions do not experience depressed voter turnout relative to states without such provisions. Second, the indirect effects of campaign finance regulations on turnout (through campaign spending and electoral competition) are contingent upon the level of any associated spending limits. Consistent with the recurring theme of this book, empirical evidence simply does not support broad generalizations about the consequences of campaign finance reform. In this respect, the indirect effects of campaign finance regulations on voter turnout depend very much on the scenario under question.

Like voter registration requirements, campaign finance regulations may serve to enhance the possibilities of electoral participation. But simply providing opportunities at either the elite level through public financing provisions or at the level of the individual citizen through eased registration requirements is probably not enough. Much still depends on the actual campaigns that are waged, the messages that are conveyed, and how candidates make use of the resources at their disposal.

# CHAPTER 8

# Campaign Finance Reform, Gubernatorial Elections, and the Political Process

In many ways, the United States is a country of contradictions, ambiguities, and uncertainties. We are a nation that firmly believes in democracy and equality, whether it be an adherence to the principle of "one person one vote" or a call to "let every vote count." At the same time, we are a nation firmly committed to the principles of capitalism, a system based upon inequality, and a belief that personal ability and hard work will result in a greater share of society's benefits. We have an innate fear of concentration of power, both corporate and governmental, yet often look to these very same institutional entities as the engines of our society. We say we value education and continue to spend more and more money on education, but remain suspicious of the "eggheads" in the "ivory towers of universities."

Americans are also impatient and pragmatic. We see a problem and want a quick solution so we can get on to the next problem. We are not a nation that excels at long-term planning or long-term disputes. Politics is seen as the art of compromise, and compromise is seen as the basis for obtaining workable solutions.

Contradictions, ambiguities, uncertainty, pragmatism, and impatience are all part of the story of campaign finance reform in America. Public opinion polls reveal that Americans are dissatisfied with the current state of campaign finance in the United States. At least in the abstract, the public overwhelmingly supports campaign finance reform.[1] Yet in the absence of scandal, reform is rarely a major issue in election campaigns. Americans are deeply suspicious of the high cost of campaigns and the perceived influence of large campaign contributors. At the same time, they seem fearful that reform may limit their First Amendment rights.[2] While compromise often serves Americans well in many areas of poli-cymaking, when it comes to campaign finance, compromise often leads to inef-fective policies and built-in loopholes that virtually invite individuals to cir-cumvent the law.

Potentially, the greatest obstacle to serious reform is American impatience and the desire to fix the problem so other matters can be addressed. As we stated in an earlier work, "Reform efforts throughout American history have followed a familiar pattern: concern over specific activities, a specific event, or set of events that helped the passage of legislation despite the reluctant support of politicos, efforts to circumvent the intent of the reform, and finally little or no enthusiasm for enforcement."[3] Interrelationships among money, elections, pol-itics, and social power have always been problematic in America and will likely remain problematic. In this sense, campaign finance reform is not an under-taking that can be completed so Americans can move on to other matters. It is a continually evolving process that involves arguments, the evaluation of evi-dence, decisions, and then reevaluation. It is in this context that we undertook the writing of this text.

We began this book by noting the lack of systematic research on the impli-cations of campaign finance reform. We do not claim that campaign finance has been understudied; the number and quality of articles, books, and confer-ence papers devoted to some aspect of campaign finance is quite substantial. In fact, there are few areas of research within the study of American politics that have developed such an impressive body of literature. Though controversies remain, we know a great deal about who gives, how much is spent, and to what effect.

Yet the ability of this work to draw substantive conclusions regarding elec-toral consequences of reform has been limited by the overwhelming focus on national elections where—until the bipartisan Campaign Reform Act of 2002—the letter of the law, though not the spirit, has remained stagnant for over twenty-five years. As a result, we know a great deal about the failures of the Fed-eral Election Campaign Act, but considerably less about how changes in the law, or different types of laws, might influence electoral behavior.

Even though most works at the state level have focused on a single state, a limited number of states over a limited time frame, or campaign spending in leg-islative elections, they can provide information about active campaign finance reform environments. In this book we attempted to overcome the limitations by turning our focus to gubernatorial elections. Because state legislators have gen-erally been more inclined to regulate gubernatorial, as opposed to legislative, campaigns, there is considerably more variance in laws across the states. Thanks to the efforts of Thad Beyle, data on gubernatorial spending patterns are avail-able from 1978 to 1998, thus offering a broad and deep pool of observations from which to draw conclusions regarding the implications of campaign finance regulations. It is our hope that this work will help to further refine future debate on campaign finance reform.

## SIZE AND POLITICS STILL MATTER

In addition to campaign finance regulations, a number of other factors help shape any given gubernatorial election. What we call geographic and political factors have important direct effects in gubernatorial elections. Very early on in this text we established that population size is a critical geographic factor in determining the cost of gubernatorial elections. It is probably safe to say that it is the most important factor. This finding is not particularly surprising. Political campaigns are, after all, about communicating a message to people, and the more people you need to contact, the greater the cost. Debates on campaign finance reform must take population into account.

The geographic size of a state is also important. Political campaigns aimed at a given number of individuals tend to be more expensive when the voters are spread out over a wider area. Nowhere in this text have we stated what the ideal gubernatorial election ought to cost. Nor would we attempt such an undertaking. The theoretical knowledge of elections and campaigns is simply insufficient to make such a claim. What we can say, however, is that any reasoned debate over the cost of gubernatorial elections must take into account population size and geographic size.

Gubernatorial elections are also conditioned by political considerations. Several findings pertaining to the considerations are significant to the debates over campaign finance reform. First, money spent by the losing candidates in a primary affects total spending, Democratic spending, Republican spending, and challenger spending. Not surprisingly, spending by losing candidates forces the eventual nominee to spend money in the primary. Candidates with one or more serious opponents in the primary, are going to have to spend more money than if they had no opponent in the primary. The importance of this finding lies in the fact that, as stated numerous times in this text, a large number of states make no distinction between the primary season and general election when it comes to campaign finance regulations. Any attempt to provide public financing and/or spending limits without a clear distinction between the primary season and general election is doomed to create large inequities between those candidates with primary opponents and those without primary opposition.

Second, incumbents tend to outspend challengers, making incumbency a dominant component of gubernatorial elections. The presence of a Democratic incumbent tends to increase Democratic spending, while the presence of a Republican incumbent tends to increase Republican spending. The presence of an incumbent also results in less competitive gubernatorial elections. In addition, the presence of a Democratic incumbent tends to result in higher Democratic vote shares. As such, failure to consider an "incumbency advantage" when proposing campaign finance reform proposals can result in significant bias.[4]

Finally, spending affects electoral competition and electoral outcomes. Democratic spending has a positive effect on the Democratic vote margin, and Republican spending has a negative effect on the Democratic vote margin. As in U.S. congressional elections, challenger spending in gubernatorial elections has a negative effect on the incumbent's vote share, while the incumbent's vote share does not seem to be affected by incumbent spending. Thus, reform proposals aimed directly at affecting spending patterns hold the potential of indirectly affecting electoral competition and electoral outcomes.

## CONTRIBUTION LIMITS, PUBLIC FINANCING, AND SPENDING LIMITS

While the importance of geographic and political factors to gubernatorial elections is interesting to examine, the primary focus of this book has been on the effects of campaign finance reform measures that have been in place in various states for various periods of time for the last twenty to twenty-five years. Although we have been unable to investigate all of the claims and counterclaims of opponents and supporters of campaign finance reform measures, one point seems clear: neither the hopes of reformers nor the fears of opponents have been fully fulfilled.

Until recently, except for some publicity laws, state reform efforts have focused mostly on contribution limits. Reform proponents generally use one or more of three basic arguments to justify contribution limits. First, proponents see contribution limits as a way to eliminate the importance of so-called fat cat contributors who lavish thousands, and in some cases millions, of dollars on their candidate of choice. At the federal level, concern over wealthy contributors was a prime motivator behind federal reform efforts in the early 1970s. Second, proponents see contribution limits as a way to stop, or at least slow down, the ever-increasing costs of running for office. Concern with the escalating costs of elections is based upon the growing public perception that the "little guy" is being squeezed out of American politics: to run for high office in America, a candidate either needs to be personally wealthy or have a group of wealthy friends. Finally, proponents see contribution limits as a way to reduce the undue influence of wealthy special interest groups and thereby further democratize the campaign finance system. The imposition of contribution limits forces candidates to seek out more and more contributors, lessening the value or importance of any single limited contribution. As such, the ability of contributors to "buy influence" becomes diminished.

Of course, the hope of contribution limit advocates is often the basis for fear on the part of opponents. First and foremost, opponents see contribution limits as an inappropriate limit on freedom of expression. Second, opponents do not see the increasing cost of elections as necessarily a problem. They argue that campaigns are about communicating to the public and any attempt to limit costs merely decreases the information available to the voting public. Third, opponents see contribution limits, in combination with the *Buckley* decision making it unconstitutional to limit the amount of money that one spends on one's own campaign, as the reason why it is more likely to have wealthy individuals run for office. Frustrated with the restrictions, candidates either spend their own money or decide not to run at all. Fourth, opponents see contribution limits as discriminatory against challengers who do not have the advantage of name recognition that incumbents have when campaign fundraising. Finally, opponents see the very democratization that supporters seek as problematic. As candidates need to seek out more and more money from a larger number of contributors, they are forced to spend more and more time on fundraising, while spending less time on more desirable activities like governing. The time and energy demands of campaign fundraising also have the unintended consequence of encouraging potential candidates to find ways to circumvent the law. In the worst-case scenario, candidates are compelled to pressure, intentionally or unintentionally, individuals or organizations to contribute to their campaign.

We simply could not address in this text all of the issues pertaining to contribution limits. Still, our analyses allow us to say unequivocally that contribution limits do not reduce the per voting age citizen cost of gubernatorial elections. Contribution limits may make it more difficult for candidates to raise money, but they apparently do not stop candidates from collecting and spending it. If the task of fundraising is more arduous, the difficulty is not reflected in campaign receipts. Funds flow regardless of whether one is considering total, Democratic, Republican, incumbent, or challenger spending. In fact, if anything, states that have more stringent regulatory environments with respect to contribution limits tend, on average, to have higher levels of spending.

Why have contribution limits failed to reduce the costs of gubernatorial elections? The answer to this question most likely involves some combination of three explanations. First, as Michael Malbin and Thomas Gais observe, enforcement of state campaign finance laws is often lax, enabling candidates and contributors to find ways to circumvent existing contribution limits.[5] Although these authors did not provide estimates of the effects of such actions, it is clear that the actions would limit the ability of contribution limits to reduce the cost of elections. Second, as campaign costs continue to rise, candidates are forced to seek larger amounts, up to the contribution limit, from individual contributors, as well as seek out a larger number of contributors. In this sense, one implication of our findings is that contribution limits may indeed be democratizing the campaign finance system.

Finally, contribution limits may simply be too high to have a significant and negative effect on campaign costs or to fundamentally alter how campaigns are conducted. The vast majority of American citizens cannot afford to contribute $500 or $1,000 to a political campaign. By definition, individuals who contribute such amounts are an economic elite, and, as such, are a limited pool of contributors.[6] Candidates may be spending more time raising money; but they still seem to have the time to raise more and more money from this limited pool. If contribution limits are lowered even further, candidates and their campaigns will likely have to spend more time raising money, a fear of opponents of contribution limits. But theoretically, at some point candidates would be unable to expend any more time raising money and limits would reduce costs.[7]

If the goal of campaign finance reform is to influence candidate spending patterns, and hence electoral outcomes, candidate-based public financing with spending limits appears to be much more promising. However, the debate over their effect continues because the combination simultaneously is the bane of reform's most vociferous opponents and the boon of its most ardent supporters. Supporters perceive the public financing component as an adrenaline shot in the arm for American democracy that promises renewed public trust (or at least reduced cynicism), more competitive elections, and greater civic participation. Opponents think spending limits are as poorly conceived as they are unconstitutional. They limit individual freedoms, thwart nonincumbent candidacies, further protect incumbents, and drive already abysmal participation rates down even further.

The reality—at least as depicted by our results—falls somewhere between the Promised Land envisioned by reformers and the democratic Hades feared by critics. Though the effects are contingent upon the level of any associated limits, as well as candidate partisanship and candidate type, public financing with spending limits does impact candidate campaign spending. It is also associated with more vulnerable incumbents and higher voter turnout. Overall, public financing of candidates with spending limits hardly has the detrimental effects so often claimed by critics. On balance, the preponderance of the evidence suggests that candidate-based public financing does more good than harm.[8]

## LOOKING TO THE FUTURE

Campaign finance reform is an issue that simply will not go away. As we complete this text, McCain–Feingold legislation has finally worked its way through Congress and now awaits federal court action, states continue to consider bold new initiatives, and federal and state court cases abound. Perhaps this is as it should be because the issues involved include some of our society's greatest concerns: free speech, equality, the integrity of our elections, our very democracy. After 225 years of practicing democracy, we still do not always know answers to questions as simple as "what is a vote?" and "how do we count them?" If these relatively simple questions remain elusive, how could we have possibly solved the inherently more complex and perhaps intractable contradiction of material inequality and political equality?

Even though it is the McCain–Feingold legislation that grabs national headlines, it is the states that serve as laboratories of democracy in regards to campaign finance reform. The ambiguities of the American public are seen in these state-level experiments. While voters in Maine, Arizona, and Massachusetts passed ballot initiatives supporting new campaign finance reform measures, voters in Oregon and Missouri voted down campaign finance reform and did so by wide margins (60–40 and 65–35, respectively). The defeats appear to have less to do with a declining faith in reform or a renewed faith in unreformed elections than with the strength and organization of the opposition. Still, they call into question any misguided view of the states as a continually fertile ground for reform. Reform may proceed at the state level, but it will do so in the presence of significant opposition. But regardless of whether reform proceeds in the states—and, if so, at what rate—there is no question that the states are now, and will continue to be, a battleground for campaign finance reform. The issue will not go away.

Likewise, the passage of the McCain–Feingold legislation at the national level hardly ends questions regarding improper influence and campaign contributions, or the buying of elections and campaign spending. These questions will return, perhaps as opponents often argue, in forms that are worse than the disease. If the history of campaign reform teaches us anything, it is that it is impossible to provide one-shot solutions to the persistent, perhaps intractable, questions that revolve around the linkages between money and political power. This lack of solutions should not, however, be taken as either an apology for the status quo or as an excuse to not engage in the process of electoral reform, but rather as an acknowledgment that reform must be thought of as a continuous process aimed at eliminating inequalities, both real and perceived, in electoral influence.

While most states (and the national government) continue to tinker with traditional proposals for reform, including publicity, contribution limits, and public financing with spending limits, other states such as Maine, Vermont, and Arizona have incorporated new and innovative thinking into their campaign finance laws.[9] All three provide public financing systems for their gubernatorial elections.

Maine is an excellent example of the new wave of innovative thinking about campaign finance. Candidates who agree to accept public funding must reject any private contributions, agree to spend none of their own money on their campaign, and agree to abide by spending limits. In order to receive public funding, a candidate must receive a given number of $5.00 qualifying contributions—50 for a State House race, 150 for a State Senate race, and 2,500 for a gubernatorial race. The qualifying contributions are not given directly to the candidate. The checks are instead made out to Maine's Clean Election fund. Candidates who agree to "run clean" receive matching funds beyond the spending limit if they are outspent by a noncompliant candidate or are the target of independent expenditures.

The advantage of the Maine approach is that it places a secondary emphasis on the traditional contribution limits which our analyses indicate are ineffective as cost control devices. While traditional contribution limits remain in place, the law effectively neutralizes their significance for candidates who agree to run clean. The fear of unfair influence accruing to campaign contributors is also minimized. In compliance with federal court decisions, acceptance of public funding is voluntary, although strong incentives are in place to encourage candidates to accept public funding.

Based on our analysis of Maine's Clean Election Act, we would expect positive effects from this act, as well as from similar legislation passed by Massachusetts, Arizona, Vermont, and other states. These effects should include a slight increase in voter turnout and incumbents becoming at least marginally more vulnerable. On this front, preliminary evidence is encouraging though not overwhelming. In both Maine and Arizona, the benefit of clean money appears to rest in public financing as a recruiting mechanism that increases the number of contested elections as well as the number of candidates running viable campaigns in both primary and general elections.[10] As one party official put it: "Even in areas where we may not win, we're going to run credible, competitive $14,000 campaigns. . . . In the past, all we could have mounted is a $200 campaign with a dozen hand-painted signs."[11] In other words, the new law has allowed public financing to step in where an unregulated campaign finance market would have failed by allowing what looked to be an uncompetitive race to remain unchallenged. While we have focused our attention on gubernatorial elections, we suspect that, to the extent that public financing serves as a tool for candidate recruitment, its effects should be much more substantial in less visible elections than in the higher profile, more visible, and harder fought gubernatorial campaigns.

Because of the *Buckley* decision, spending limits and candidate-based public financing have become linked in a way that makes it virtually impossible to analyze the independent effects of these two measures. Nevertheless, the preponderance of evidence suggests that the combination of public financing and spending limits does, overall, have positive consequences. Because of data limitations we do not know how many gubernatorial candidates accepted public financing and spending limits and how many opted for complete private financing.[12] We suspect that our results would have been even more favorable for the reformist agenda had all candidates accepted public financing.

For public financing to work, it is critical that states maximize the incentive structure to encourage acceptance of public funding and associated spending limits. Both Maine and Kentucky are states that provide the types of incentives that other states ought to consider. And yet, the Kentucky law that worked well in 1995 with an open seat fell considerably short of the reformist ideal in 1999 when a popular incumbent ran for reelection. Likewise, the 2002 gubernatorial election was a test of Maine's law, as candidates considered opting out of the public financing provisions because public funding is based on the average spent in the last two election cycles, and this average was driven down by an uncompetitive 1998 gubernatorial election featuring popular incumbent Angus King. As a result, clean money public subsidies may not be high enough to entice compliance, and may even put clean money candidates at a considerable disadvantage.[13]

Rather than reject all campaign finance regulations, we should acknowledge their limitations. Even good laws fail on occasion. And there is much in any given election cycle that is beyond the reach of laws that serve not as the principal player but as part of the electoral backdrop. If we believe that reform will cleanse politics of all vestiges of interested money and of all perceptions of corruption, while at the same time moving American democracy closer to the liberal ideal of participatory, competitive, and issue oriented elections, then reform is sure to fail. But if we ask in what ways are differences in campaign finance regulations associated with different electoral outcomes, we can begin to develop some answers that speak directly to the impact of the law.

From our analysis, we conclude that, if the goal of reform is to influence candidate spending, electoral outcomes, and voter turnout, the best mechanism for affecting change is a combination of candidate-based public financing and spending limits. Contribution limits appear less effective, but could be used as a mechanism for encouraging compliance with public financing provisions. The lower the contribution limits, the greater the incentive for candidates to accept public financing and associated spending limits.

Regardless of whether one accepts our conclusions, this much seems beyond dispute: the debate over campaign finance reform will continue and further analysis will be necessary as states continue their bold experiments in the world of campaign finance regulation.

# Notes

## NOTES TO INTRODUCTION

1. According to a Washington Post/ABC News Poll, 30 percent of respondents indicated that reforming election campaign finance laws would be "very important" in the 2000 presidential election. An additional 40 percent said the issue would be "somewhat important." Only 11 percent said that campaign finance reform would be "not important at all." The poll was based on 1,526 random telephone interviews conducted between August 30 and September 2, 1999.

2. Before the passage of McCain–Feingold, Congress voted to require that so-called 527s disclose donors. 527s are organizations, designated by the IRS tax code, that do not engage in electoral advocacy. Named after a provision in the tax code, 527s became politically popular because the groups did not have to disclose the identity of donors or the size of the contributions to the FEC, provided that they did not advocate the defeat or election of any specific candidate. Notably, this change was the first major one in campaign finance law in over two decades. The impact of the change is unclear. For one thing, the new law will not affect some groups operating under certain provisions of the tax code. In addition, the legislation does not stipulate when the disclosure of donors is supposed to occur. Finally, the law is likely to be subject to constitutional challenge. See, for example, Mike Allen, "Campaign Secrecy Law's Impact Doubted," *Washington Post*, 1 July 2000, A6.

3. For a discussion of the importance of soft money in congressional elections, see David Magelby, *Outside Money: Soft Money and Issue Advocacy in the 1998 Congressional Elections* (Boulder, Colo.: Rowman & Littlefield, 2000).

4. Of course, the consequences of McCain–Feingold depend upon the outcome of any court challenges which opponents, such as Mitch McConnell, have vowed to undertake. McCain–Feingold changed one major hard money component of federal law: contribution limits were increased and indexed to inflation. The Bookings Institute provides what is perhaps the best summary of the McCain–Feingold legislation, as well as recent developments in campaign finance. See, www. Brodc.edu/dybdoc/oot/gs/cf/cf_hp.htm.

5. See Robert Dreyfuss, "Reform beyond the Beltway: States as Laboratories of Clean Money," *American Prospect* 31 (1998): 50–55.

6. In the 2000 elections, clean money proposals in Missouri and Oregon were easily defeated. It is unclear whether their defeat means the momentum for reform has died down, or whether the opposition is now better organized.

7. See David Beiler, "The Body Politic Registers a Protest," *Campaigns and Elections* 20 (1999): 34–43.

8. Ibid.

9. See Steven Schier, "Jesse's Victory," *Washington Monthly* 31 (1999): 8–13.

10. In 1996 these limits were raised to $1,000 for any one election.

11. Unlike in most states, Kentucky makes a clear legal distinction between the funding period for the primary election and the funding period for the general election. As such, a

candidate cannot receive any contribution later than 28 days before the May primary. After the primary is over, a new accounting period starts and the candidate can once again receive contributions until 28 days before the November general election.

12. In many respects, the Registry in Kentucky has similar responsibilities to that of the Federal Election Commission, which has jurisdiction over federal elections.

13. The minimum threshold and maximum state subsidy are also adjusted by the consumer price index before each gubernatorial election.

14. Prior to the amendment, Kentucky governors were limited to one four-year term.

15. See, for example, Frank Sorauf, *Inside Campaign Finance Reform: Myths and Realities* (New Haven, Conn.: Yale University Press, 1992); Frank Sorauf, *Money in American Elections* (Glenview, Ill.: Scott, Foresman, 1988); Gary Jacobson, *Money in Congressional Elections* (New Haven, Conn.: Yale University Press, 1980); Alan Abramowitz, "Incumbency, Campaign Spending, and the Decline of Competition in U.S. House Elections," *Journal of Politics* 53 (1991): 34–56; Donald Green and Jonathan Krasno, "Salvation for the Spendthrift Incumbent," *American Journal of Political Science* 32 (1988): 844–907; Robert Goidel, Donald Gross, and Todd Shields, *Money Matters: Consequences of Campaign Finance Reform in U.S. House Elections* (Lanham, Md., Rowman & Littlefield, 1999).

16. See Patrick Donnay and Graham Ramsden, "Public Financing of Legislative Elections: Lessons from Minnesota," *Legislative Studies Quarterly* 20 (1995): 351–64; Kenneth Mayer and John Wood, "The Impact of Public Financing on Electoral Competitiveness: Evidence from Wisconsin, 1964–1990," *Legislative Studies Quarterly* 20 (1995): 69–88; Kenneth Mayer, "Campaign Finance Reform in the States: A Report to the Governor's Blue Ribbon Commission on Campaign Finance Reform" (unpublished paper, 1997); Joel Thompson and Gary Moncrief, eds., "*Campaign Finance in State Legislative Elections* (Washington, D.C.: Congressional Quarterly Press, 1998); Kent Redfield, "The Good, the Bad, and the Perfect: Searching for Campaign Finance Reform in Illinois," *Spectrum: Journal of State Government* 69 (1996): 38–42.

17. See Thompson and Moncrief, *Campaign Finance in State Legislative Elections*; Kenneth Mayer, *Campaign Finance Reform in the States;* Michael Mablin and Thomas Gais, *The Day after Reform: Sobering Campaign Finance Lessons from the American States* (Albany, N.Y.: Rockefeller Institute Press, 1998); Robert Hogan, "Campaign Spending in State Legislative Primary Elections," *State and Local Government Review* 31 (1999): 214–40; Robert Hogan, "The Costs of Representation in State Legislatures: Explaining Variations in Campaign Spending," *Social Science Quarterly* (forthcoming).

18. See Malcolm Jewell and William Cassie, "Can the Legislative Campaign Finance System Be Reformed?" in Thompson and Moncrief, *Campaign Finance in State Legislative Elections.*

19. Robert Hogan, "The Costs of Representation in State Legislatures."

20. See, for example, Jacobson, *Money in Congressional Elections*; Green and Krasno, "Salvation for the Spendthrift Incumbent"; Goidel, Gross, and Shields, *Money Matters*; Thompson and Moncrief, *Campaign Finance in State Legislative Elections.*

21. In fact, until recently, there has been very little research examining the impact of gubernatorial campaign spending on either electoral outcomes or voter turnout, but see Samuel Patterson, "Campaign Spending in the Contest for Governor," *Western Political Quarterly* 35 (1982): 457–77; Samuel Patterson and Gregory Caldeira, "Getting Out the Vote: Participation in Gubernatorial Elections," *American Political Science Review* 77 (1983): 675–99; Craig Svoboda, "How and Why Voters Vote in Gubernatorial Elections" (Ph.D. dissertation University of Wisconsin-Milwaukee, 1995).

22. See Randall Partin, "Assessing the Impact of Campaign Spending in Governors Races" (paper presented at the annual meeting of the American Political Science Association, Atlanta, Ga., September 1999). It should be noted that in the congressional elections literature the marginal effect of incumbent campaign spending remains in dispute; see, for example, Donald Green and Jonathan Krasno, "Salvation for the Spendthrift Incumbent."

23. See Peverill Squire and Christina Fastnow, "Comparing Gubernatorial and Senatorial Elections," *Political Research Quarterly* 47 (1994): 703–20; Kim Kahn, "Characteristics of Press Coverage in Senate and Gubernatorial Elections: Information Available to Voters," *Legislative Studies Quarterly* 20 (1995): 1–23; Peverill Squire, "Challenger Profile and Gubernatorial Elections," *Western Political Quarterly* 45 (1992): 124–42.

24. See Anthony Gierzynski, "Data Gathering Issues," in Thompson and Moncrief, *Campaign Finance in State Legislative Elections,* for a discussion of the problems in obtaining data on state legislative campaign finance and creating comparable data records.

25. Thad Beyle graciously provided the data on gubernatorial spending, to which we added data on spending in Senate elections, state campaign finance laws, and state demographics. See his "Big Spending in the Quest for the Governor's Chair, *State Government* 65 (1992): 15–20;"The Cost of Becoming Governor," *State Government* 59 (1986): 95–101; and "The Cost of Becoming Governor," *State Government* 56 (1983): 74–84.

## NOTES TO CHAPTER 1

1. Prior to the passage of the McCain–Feingold legislation, the only change in federal campaign finance laws in more than two decades was the requirement that tax code section 527 groups disclose donors. We contend that the change is relatively minor, though our characterization is certainly subject to dispute.

2. The tendency to focus on the national-level debate over campaign finance issues exists among the public and academics alike. Two important exceptions to this tendency are the works by Malbin and Gais, *The Day after Reform;* and Thompson and Moncrief, *Campaign Finance in State Legislative Elections.*

3. The state alone has the authority to regulate state elections, such as those for governor and the state legislature. In the case of federal elections to the U.S. House and Senate, state and federal powers are concurrent. States, for example, regulate primaries.

4. Forty-eight of the states have four-year gubernatorial terms of office and forty-nine states allow an incumbent governor to run for reelection at least once.

5. For a more complete history of campaign finance in the United States that focuses on nationwide developments, see chapter 2 in Goidel, Gross, and Shields, *Money Matters.*

6. There can be little doubt that the Watergate scandal of 1972–73 was the turning point in the debate over campaign finance regulations. After Watergate, the entire campaign finance system became the focus of national debate, and in 1974 Congress passed a series of provisions that represented the most comprehensive effort to reform and regulate campaign finance in our nation's history. Many states soon followed suit and reformed their state campaign finance systems. Of equal importance is the fact that comprehensive reform remains part of the public agenda with numerous states experimenting with different reform packages. See Goidel, Gross, and Shields, *Money Matters,* 25–34.

7. In his first campaign for office, George Washington was said to have used liquor as a means to attract voters. See George Thayer, *Who Shakes the Money Tree* (New York: Simon & Schuster, 1973), 25.

8. The transportation of voters to the polls remains problematic in a number of states. In their book *Dirty Little Secrets* (New York: Random House, 1996), Larry Sabato and Glenn Simpson discuss problems associated with the use of so-called street money or walking around money.

9. The Tammany Hall campaign fund, for example, received 6 percent of all New York City employees' weekly paychecks.

10. Civil service reform and attacks on the assessment system were critical components of the Progressive movement.

11. See Herbert Alexander and Laura Denny, *Regulation of Political Finance* (Princeton, N.J.: Citizens Research Foundation, 1966), 13.

12. The link between the economically rich and powerful and needy candidates and political parties had been forged during the first half of the nineteenth century.

13. Scandals contributed to public cynicism. One national-level scandal, for example, found that a number of the nation's largest insurance companies had been using policyholders' money for various political purposes.

14. See Louise Overacker, *Money in Elections* (New York: Macmillan, 1932), 294.

15. In some cases, states prohibited contributions from only particular types of corporations, such as regulated industries.

16. See Alexander and Denny, *Regulation of Political Finance,* 12.

17. While the number of PACs began to increase during the 1950s and 1960s, their great expansion is really a post-1970 development. A brief discussion of the development and growth of PACs can be found in chapter 4 of Sorauf's *Money in American Elections.*

18. Amendments to the Tillman Act placed expenditure limits of $5,000 and $10,000 on U.S. House and Senate campaigns, respectively. The Corrupt Practices Act of 1925 raised these limits to between $10,000 and $25,000 for U.S. Senate races and between $2,500 and $5,000 for U.S. House races.

19. One of the ongoing problems in such laws are questions of how one determines what is meant by acting on behalf of a candidate and who is responsible for controlling such activities. There are also fundamental legal and constitutional questions underlying such laws. For example, in 1916 the Wisconsin Supreme Court invalidated a law which attempted to regulate expenditures on behalf of a candidate (see Alexander and Denny, *Regulation of Political Finance,* 18).

20. See, for example, Overacker, *Money in Elections,* and Alexander and Denny, *Regulation of Political Finance.* Perhaps the greatest success involved limits on bribery, but even here problems often emerged.

21. Colorado, Florida, Montana, Oregon, North Dakota, South Dakota, and Wyoming all had such laws.

22. See, for example, Overacker, *Money in Elections,* and Alexander and Denny, *Regulation of Political Finance.*

23. Overacker, *Money in Elections,* 291.

24. According to Overacker (*Money in Elections,* 327), in 1932 five states (Georgia, Maine, Montana, Nevada, and Oregon) published either campaign reports or summary campaign analyses.

25. Teddy Roosevelt and the Progressives stand as a notable exception.

26. Minnesota, for example, extends disclosure requirements to financial intermediaries, such as "bundlers" and "solicitors." Bundlers are individuals or organizations that collect contributions and then hand them over to a candidate. Solicitors are individuals who convince others to contribute to a candidate. An increasing number of states require reports from organizations or individuals who engage in independent expenditures.

27. In the most comprehensive analysis of disclosure laws to date, Malbin and Gais report numerous difficulties in the operation of state-level disclosure laws. They report difficulties in the quality and integrity of the information that is received, in making useful information public; and in the use of information by the public. See Malbin and Gais, *The Day after Reform.*

28. During the 1990s, an increasing number of states also placed contribution restrictions on the candidates themselves, the candidate's family, and regulated industries. In fact, forty-seven states place some limit on contributions to gubernatorial campaigns from regulated industries.

29. See Malbin and Gais, *The Day after Reform,* 15–21.

30. Ibid.

31. Four states, Kentucky, Minnesota, North Carolina, and Rhode Island, provide public money to political parties and candidates. See Malbin and Gais, *The Day after Reform,* for a discussion of the various forms of public financing in American states.

32. It is not at all clear that the strategic allocation of contributions, among any set of contributors, necessarily results in higher average levels of competition, particularly if contributors engage in an access rather than an electoral strategy. See, for example, Goidel, Gross, and Shields, *Money Matters.*

33. Disparities in spending are most likely to be seen when there is an incumbent in the election. See, for example, Keith Gaddie, "Forgotten Races: Open Seat Congressional Elections" (unpublished manuscript, 1997).

34. *Buckley v. Valeo,* 424 U.S. 1 (1976).

35. See, for example, Joshua Rosenkranz, *Buckley Stops Here: Loosening the Judicial Stranglehold on Campaign Finance Reform* (Washington, D.C.: Twentieth Century Fund, 1998); and Burt Neuborne, *Campaign Finance Reform and the Constitution: A Critical Look at* Buckley v. Valeo (New York: Brennan Center for Justice, 1998).

36. A current court case in Vermont is testing this proposition.

37. Court challenges could reduce this number by the time of publication.

## NOTES TO CHAPTER 2

1. See Sorauf, *Inside Campaign Finance Reform,* 7.

2. Ibid., 28.

3. See Bradley Smith. "Faulty Assumptions and Undemocratic Consequences of Campaign Finance Reform," *Yale Law Journal* 105 (1995): 1049–91.

4. Ibid., 142.

5. See Ellen Miller and Joshua Rosenkranz, "How Was Campaign-Finance Reform Killed? By Twisting What the High Court Said: Free Speech and Campaign Myth," *Nation* 266 (27 April 1998): 22–25.

6. See Elizabeth Drew, *The Corruption of American Politics: What Went Wrong and Why* (Secaucus, N.J.: Carol Publishing Group, 1999), 143.

7. Ibid., 165.

8. See, for example, Rosenkranz, *Buckley Stops Here;* and Neuborne, *Campaign Finance Reform and the Constitution.*

9. See Michael Crowley and Frank Phillips, "Mass. House Waters Down Key Reforms," *Boston Globe,* 15 April 2000, A1.

10. See "The People's Will," *Boston Globe,* 11 May 2000, A26.

11. See "Democrats Behaving Badly," *Boston Globe,* 6 June 2000, A14.

12. See Brooks Jackson, *Broken Promises: Why the Federal Election Commission Failed* (New York: Priority Press, 1990).

13. See Donnay and Ramsden, "Public Financing of Legislative Elections"; and Mayer, *Campaign Finance Reform in the States.*

14. See Mayer and Wood, "Impact of Public Financing on Electoral Competitiveness"; and Mayer, *Campaign Finance Reform in the States.*

15. For a fuller account of voter information levels and their implications, see Michael X. Delli Carpini and Scott Keeter, *What Americans Know and Why It Matters* (New Haven, Conn.: Yale University, 1996).

16. See, for example, chapter 7 in Goidel, Gross, and Shields, *Money Matters.*

17. See Sabato and Simpson, *Dirty Little Secrets,* 7.

18. See Henry Chappell, "Campaign Contributions and Congressional Voting: A Simultaneous Probit-Tobit Model," *Review of Economic and Statistics* 62 (1982): 77–83; William Welch, "Campaign Contributions and Legislative Voting: Milk Money and Dairy Supports," *Western Political Quarterly* 35 (1982): 478–95; John Wright, "PACs, Contributions, and Roll Calls: An Organizational Perspective," *American Political Science Review* 79 (1985): 400–14; John Wright, "Contributions, Lobbying, and Committee Voting in the U.S. House of Representatives," *American Political Science Review* 84 (1990): 417–38; John Wright, *Interest Groups and Congress: Lobbying, Contributions, and Influence* (Boston: Allyn & Bacon, 1996); Janet Grenzke, "Shopping in the Congressional Supermarket: The Currency Is Complex," *American Journal of Political Science* 33 (1990): 1–24; Diana Evans, "PAC Contributions and Roll Call Voting: Conditional Power," in *Interest Group Politics,* 2d. ed., edited by Allan Cigler and Burdette Loomis (Washington, D.C.: Congressional Quarterly Press, 1986); Woodrow Jones and K. Robert Keiser, "Issue Visibility and the Effects of PAC Money," *Social Science Quarterly* 68 (1987): 170–76; Jean Schroedel, "Campaign Contributions and Legislative Outcomes," *Western Political Quarterly* 40 (1987): 371–89; Lawrence Rothenberg, *Linking Citizens to Government: Interest Group Politics at Common Cause* (New York: Cambridge University Press, 1992); and Laura Langbein and Mark Lotwis, "The Political Efficacy of Lobbying and Money: Gun Control in the U.S. House," *Legislative Studies Quarterly* 14 (1990): 414–40.

19. For a defense of anecdotal evidence and a criticism of the statistical evidence, see Daniel Hays Lowenstein, "On Campaign Finance Reform: The Root of All Evil Is Deeply Rooted," *Hofstra Law Review* 18 (1989): 301.

20. *Buckley v. Valeo,* 27.

21. See statement of Sen. William Proxmire quoted in *Congressional Record,* 132d Cong., S11, 163 (11 August 1986).

22. See Wright, "Contributions, Lobbying, and Committee Voting."

23. See Wright, "Contributions, Lobbying, and Committee Voting"; and *Interest Groups and Congress.*

24. See Darrell West and Burdett Loomis, *The Sound of Money: How Political Interests Get What They Want* (New York: W.W. Norton, 1998), 223.

25. Ibid., 224.

26. *Nixon v. Shrink Missouri Government PAC,* 161 F3d 519 (2000), 15.

27. See Steven Rosenstone and John Hansen, *Mobilization, Participation, and Democracy in America* (New York: Macmillin, 1993); and Sydney Verba, Kay Schlozman, and Henry Brady, *Voice and Equality: Civic Voluntarism in American Politics* (Boston: Harvard University Press, 1995).

28. See John Green, Paul Herrnson, Lynda Powell, and Clyde Wilcox, "Individual Con-

gressional Campaign Contributors: Wealthy, Conservative and Reform-Minded" (unpublished manuscript, 2001; available on the internet at *www.bsos.umd.edu*. The research was funded by the Joyce Foundation).

29. See Todd Shields and Robert Goidel, "Who Contributes?: Checkbook Participation, Class Biases, and the Impact of Legal Reforms, 1952–1994," *American Politics Quarterly* 28 (2000): 216–33. More recent evidence suggests that women may be playing a larger role in campaign finance; see John Green, Paul Herrnson, Lynda Powell, and Clyde Wilcox, "Women, Big Donors Mobilized in Congressional Elections" (unpublished manuscript 1999, available on the internet at *www.bsos.umd.edu*. The research was funded by the Joyce Foundation).

30. The dramatic jump in 1976 reflects question wording. In the survey for that year, individuals who opted for the tax check-off were included as contributors.

31. See Smith, "Faulty Assumptions"; and Michael J. Malbin, "Most GOP Winners Spent Enough Money to Reach Voters," *Political Finance and Lobby Reporter* (11 January 1995).

32. See Janet Box-Steffensmeier, "A Dynamic Analysis of the Role of War Chests in Campaign Strategy," *American Journal of Political Science* 40 (1996): 352–71; and Robert Goidel and Donald Gross, "A Systems Approach to Campaign Finance in U.S. House Elections," *American Politics Quarterly* 22 (1994): 125–53.

33. See Ruth Jones, "Financing State Elections," in Michael Malbin, ed., *Money and Politics in the United States: Financing Elections in the 1980s* (Chatham, N.J.: Chatham House, 1984).

34. See Malcolm Jewell and David Olson, *Political Parties and Elections in American States,* 3d ed. (Chicago: Dorsey Press, 1988).

35. See Jewell and Olson, *Political Parties and Elections*; Jones, "Financing State Elections"; and Ruth Jones, "U.S. State-Level Campaign Finance Reform," in Herbert Alexander and Rei Shiratori, *Comparative Political Finance among the Democracies* (Boulder, Colo.: Westview Press, 1994).

36. See Neuborne, *Campaign Finance Reform and the Constitution.*

37. Ibid.

38. Ibid., 26.

39. *Buckley v. Valeo,* 92–93.

40. See Deborah Goldberg, *Writing Reform: A Guide to Drafting State and Local Campaign Finance Laws* (New York: Brennan Center for Justice, 1998).

41. Ibid.

42. See Malbin and Gais, *The Day after Reform.*

43. See Jewell and Cassie, "Can the Legislative Campaign Finance System Be Reformed?"

44. See, for example, Jacobson, *Money in Congressional Elections.*

45. See Green and Krasno, "Salvation for the Spendthrift Incumbent," 844–907.

## NOTES TO CHAPTER 3

1. See Gierzynski, *Money Rules;* Gerald M. Pomper, *The Election of 2000* (New York: Chatham House Publishers, 2001); and Paul S. Herrnson, *Congressional Elections: Campaigning at Home and in Washington,* 2d ed. (Washington, D.C.: Congressional Quarterly Press, 1998).

2. Throughout this book we focus on hard-money considerations. Until the mid-1990s, most research documenting the ever-increasing costs of elections has focused on hard money expenditures. If one were to consider soft money and independent expenditures, the rates of increase in campaign spending would be much higher than typically reported. For example,

it appears that soft money and other types of noncandidate expenditures in the year 2000 congressional, senate, and presidential races often equaled or exceeded candidates' hard money expenditures. See David Magelby, *Election Advocacy: Soft Money and Issue Advocacy in the 2000 Congressional Elections,* report funded by the Pew Charitable Trusts (Salt Lake City: Brigham Young University, 2001).

3. Throughout this chapter we focus on the total amount of money spent in gubernatorial campaigns; that is, money spent in both the primary and general elections. One of the difficulties of analyzing spending in gubernatorial elections is that in some states there is a clear distinction between the monies that are spent in the primary and those spent in the general election, while in a large number of states there is no statutory distinction between the monies spent in a primary and those spent in the general election. Since we are mostly concerned in this chapter with setting out the overall parameters of spending in gubernatorial elections, we focus on the total amount of money spent in both primary and general gubernatorial elections.

4. Of this total, approximately $53 million was spent in the general election by the two major party candidates.

5. The thirteen states were: Alabama, Alaska, Arizona, California, Georgia, Illinois, Indiana, Maine, Minnesota, Nebraska, New Hampshire, Ohio, and Rhode Island.

6. These numbers represent total spending in actual dollar amounts. Of course, a good amount of this increase can be attributed to inflation effects over the period. Nevertheless, the 1998 election period represented a 215 percent increase of the 1978 period when measured in constant 1992 dollars.

7. One way to view the diversity among the states over the time period is to consider some descriptive statistics. For the thirty-six states that had gubernatorial elections in 1978, the mean cost was $2,732,136, with a standard deviation of $2,882,031. For the thirty-six that had gubernatorial elections in 1998, by contrast, the mean cost was approximately $13,000,000, with a standard deviation of $11,139,248.

8. When evaluating these averages, it must be remembered that both Vermont and New Hampshire are counted twice because they have gubernatorial elections every two years.

9. The four-year average was used to insure that the same states were used whenever making comparisons. If the four-year average were not used, there would be large fluctuations when moving from one year to the next merely because of the inclusion or exclusion of very large states such as California and New York.

10. Constant 1992 dollars are used throughout this text to control for the effects of inflation.

11. Even though all congressional elections are held every two years, averages were computed over a four-year period, or two sets of congressional elections. This double computation was done to insure greater compatibility with the four-year cycle used to compute gubernatorial averages. Also, it is well known that the cost of running for congress differs between the presidential election year and the off-year (see Goidel, Gross, and Shields, *Money Matters*). Computing averages over four years diminishes the effects of fluctuations resulting from the presidential election year-off-year cycle.

12. Senate averages are computed over a six-year period simply because it takes six years to insure that all of the states are included in the computations for a given data point. If the average were computed for just a two- or four-year period, then major fluctuations from one year to the next would likely be seen simply because of the particular subset of states used to compute any two- or four-year average.

13. Pearson correlations are used in this analysis. See Hubert M. Blalock, *Social Statistics* (New York: McGraw-Hill, 1979).

14. The actual equation used to evaluate these trends lines was:
$$Y = \alpha + \beta X + \varepsilon$$
where:

    $Y$ = the average statewide expenditure for a given type of office for a given year;

    $X$ = a counter from 0 to 17 associated with each year, 1981 = 0, 1982 = 1, 1983 = 2, etc.

15. For example, it could be the case that gubernatorial elections in state A cost $80 million in 1994 and $100 million in 1998, while the state's U.S. Senate elections cost $10 million and $20 million in 1994 and 1998, respectively. State B's cost of gubernatorial elections might be $60 million in 1994 and $70 million in 1998, while its Senate costs might be $12 million and $22 million in 1998. Under such conditions, the average cost of both types of elections increased from 1994 to 1998, but state A had more expensive gubernatorial elections, while state B had more expensive U.S. Senate elections.

16. In order to match up the elections for the correlation analysis, the statewide totals for the most recent set of U.S. House elections were used in the analysis if a state did not have a U.S. House election in the same year as a gubernatorial election. Likewise, if the state did not have a U.S. Senate election for the state's senior senator in the same year as a gubernatorial election, then the most recent U.S. Senate election for the position was used in the analysis. The correlations are based on 62 to 93 cases. The correlation between spending in gubernatorial elections and spending in senate elections in those cases where there were concurrent gubernatorial and senate elections during the time period is .73.

17. The six states with the largest populations in the United States are California, Florida, Illinois, New York, Pennsylvania, and Texas.

18. The seven least populated states are Alaska, Delaware, Montana, North Dakota, South Dakota, Vermont, and Wyoming. Of these seven, only Alaska does not show up as having one of the twenty least expensive gubernatorial elections. It should also be noted that seven of the twenty least expensive gubernatorial campaigns occurred in Vermont.

19. See Goidel, Gross, and Shields, *Money Matters.*

20. Five of the last seven U.S. presidents came from two of the six largest states: Nixon and Reagan from California and Johnson and both Bushes from Texas.

21. There is no exact method for determining the hypothetical pool of contributors, nor is it possible to determine the hypothetical amount of money that might be contributed. As the importance of out-of-state money grows, these unknowns become even harder to determine.

22. The total cost of gubernatorial elections is based upon constant 1992 dollars spent by all candidates in the primary and general elections. Population is measured in terms of the voting age population of a state. Total state personal income is based upon estimates from the U.S. Department of Commerce. Geographic size is merely the size of the state measured in total square miles.

23. The constant and the coefficient associated with the geographic size variable are statistically significant at the .001 level. The coefficient associated with the income per voting age citizen is not statistically significant at the .05 level ($p$ = .53). The r-squared value for the entire equation is .27.

24. If one were to compare the standardized regression coefficients for equation 3.1, the standardized coefficient associated with the geographic size variable is .51, while the standardized coefficient associated with the income variable is .03. If one were to add a series of twenty dummy variables, one for each year minus one, to equation 3.1 in order to take into account the effect of time, the coefficients associated with income and geographic size are not significantly changed from those seen in equation 3.1. For a discussion of the use of standardized variables to compare the importance of variables in a regression equation, see Donald A.

Gross, "Problems in Making Meaningful Comparisons: A Research Note," *Humbolt Journal of Social Relations* 8 (1981).

25. In fact, the correlation between total spending per voting age citizen in gubernatorial elections and personal income per voting age citizens is .02, which is not significant at the 0.10 level of significance. The correlation between the geographic size of a state and the total spending per voting age citizen in gubernatorial elections is .52, which is significant at the 0.001 level of significance.

26. If one only considers those senate elections which were held concurrently with gubernatorial elections, the correlation between the cost of gubernatorial elections per voting age citizen and the cost of senatorial elections per voting age citizen is .02 and not statistically significant. None of the correlations in table 3.5 associated with gubernatorial spending are statistically significant at the .10 level.

27. We also examined the importance of two other indicators of the overall economic well-being of a state to the cost of elections: the poverty rate and the unemployment rate. In neither case did they have a statistically significant effect on the per voting age citizen cost of gubernatorial elections, U.S. senate elections, or U.S. house elections.

28. Our analysis reinforces the arguments made by Partin (see "Assessing the Impact of Campaign Spending in Governors' Races").

29. It is not clear why geographic size had a positive and statistically significant effect on elections for the senior senator's position and is not statistically significant, although still positive, in the case of elections for the junior senator's position.

## NOTES TO CHAPTER 4

1. There are individuals who do not see the rising costs of electoral campaigns as being especially problematic. In fact, there are those who would argue that, if anything, we ought to spend even more money on campaigns in America. For a discussion of these alternative views, see Smith, "Faulty Assumptions"; and Sorauf, *Money in American Elections*, 367–69.

2. See Malbin and Gais, *The Day after Reform.*

3. See Jewell and Cassie, "Can the Legislative Campaign Finance System Be Reformed?"

4. Works which suggest the negative consequences of reform include: Sorauf, *Inside Campaign Finance Reform;* Jacobson, *Money in Congressional Elections;* and Abramowitz, "Incumbency, Campaign Spending, and the Decline of Competition in U.S. House Elections," 34–56. Works that provide a more positive assessment include: Green and Krasno, "Salvation for the Spendthrift Incumbent," 844–907; Jonathan S. Krasno and Donald P. Green, "Stopping the Buck Here: The Case for Campaign Spending Limits," *Brookings Review* (1993): 17–21; Robert K. Goidel and Donald A. Gross, "Reconsidering the Myths and Realities of Campaign Finance Reform," *Legislative Studies Quarterly* 21 (1996): 129–50; and Goidel, Gross, and Shields, *Money Matters.*

5. While our data set theoretically includes all gubernatorial elections for all states from 1978 to 1998, there are some missing data for some of our variables.

6. See *Buckley v. Valeo.* In all of the cases in which there are effective spending limits, one also finds public financing to candidates. In order to comply with court directives, public financing and other incentives are used to entice candidates into accepting spending limits.

7. While there are some violations, the contribution limits index conforms to a Guttman scale. The coefficient of reproducibility is .98, while the coefficient of scalability is

.93. For a discussion of cumulative Guttman scaling, see John McIver and Edward Carmines, *Unidimensional Scaling* (Beverly Hills, Calif.: Sage Publications, 1981).

8. We also tried a number of alternative specifications for the contribution limit data. We tried placing the arbitrary contribution limit for states without actual contribution limit laws at $500,000. We tried taking the square root and logs of the two sets of contribution limits before running the correlations. And we tried setting the contribution limits on a per voter basis for the various specifications. In no case were the substantive conclusions significantly changed by the alternative specifications.

9. See Malbin and Gais, *The Day after Reform*, 106–30.

10. See Gierzynski, *Money Rules,* 26–27.

11. Using total spending by the losing candidates in the primary to analyze gubernatorial election costs is preferable to using the number of candidates in the primary because it is the financial competitiveness that is more likely to increase spending by the eventual nominee rather than the mere presence of potential challengers.

12. The ability of congressional incumbents to scare off serious challengers is one of many advantages they enjoy. See Peverill Squire, "Preemptive Fundraising and Challenger Profile in Senate Elections," *Journal of Politics* 53 (1991): 1150–64; and Steffensmeier, "A Dynamic Analysis of the Role of War Chests," 352–71.

13. See Goidel, Gross, and Shields, *Money Matters;* Sorauf, *Inside Campaign Finance Reform;* and Jacobson, *Money in Congressional Elections.*

14. The exact nature of the relationship between political competition and campaign spending has been the subject of great debate. While there is general agreement that more competitive elections tend to be more expensive, the causal nature and specification of the factors that underlie the relationship have been extensively debated. See Goidel, Gross, and Shields, *Money Matters,* chapter 4.

15. Competition is an index based on the Democratic percentage of the vote in the most recent presidential and U.S. Senate campaigns and the Democratic percentage of the state senate and state house. The index is similar to that developed by Austin Ranney (see "Parties in State Politics," in *Politics in the American States,* 3d ed., edited by Herbert Jacob and Kenneth Vines [Boston: Little, Brown & Co., 1976]). We did not use the actual Ranney index because it uses outcomes in gubernatorial elections and we wanted a measure of the overall competitive environment outside of the current gubernatorial election. We began by developing a partisanship variable representing the average level of Democratic success in the five settings stated above. The partisanship variable is merely the sum of the five percentages divided by five. We then folded the index such that:

COMPETITION = absolute value of [partisanship – (100 – partisanship)]

where lower values indicate more competitive states. For a review of the literature on electoral competition see Thomas Holbrook and Emily Van Dunk, "Electoral Competition in the American States," *American Political Science Review* 87 (1993): 955–62.

16. Gary Jacobson and Samuel Kernell, *Strategy and Choice in Congressional Elections,* 2d ed. (New Haven, Conn.: Yale University Press, 1983). While we include year dummy variables to control for the electoral context, we do not provide substantive interpretations for the variables.

17. Including the dummy variables for separate years also controls for differences in presidential versus nonpresidential years, as well as for states that hold gubernatorial elections in odd numbered years.

18. In order for any of the contribution limit variables to be included in the equations, an arbitrarily high value would have had to be assigned to those states not having contribution

limits. The designation of such a value would have made all six of the contribution limit variables highly colinear, with the resultant estimates being highly unstable.

19. See Redfield, "The Good, the Bad, and the Perfect," 38–42; and Sorauf, *Inside Campaign Finance Reform.*

20. Pooled time series data present several problems to OLS estimation including potential problems with heteroscedasticity, usually associated with cross-sectional data, and autocorrelation, generally associated with time series data. See James Stimson, "Regression in Space and Time: A Statistical Essay," *American Journal of Political Science* 29 (1985): 914–47; and Louis Sayrs, *Pooled Time Series Analysis* (Newbury Park, Calif.: Sage Publications, 1989). While GLS has traditionally been used in pooled time series applications, Beck and Katz contend that GLS estimators understate the variability of the standard errors. Using Monte Carlo experiments, Nathaniel Beck and Jonathan N. Katz contend that instead of GLS, pooled time series models should be estimated using OLS with panel-corrected standard errors. The pooled time series estimates presented in this text are computed using OLS with panel-corrected standard errors (using STATA), under the assumption of heteroscedasticity across states. See Beck and Katz, "What to Do (and Not to Do) with Time-Series Cross-Section Data," *American Political Science Review* 89 (1995): 634–47.

21. While the dummy variables for each year are not included in the table for ease of interpretation, it should be noted that in four cases the coefficient was positive and statistically significant at the .05 level: 1983, 1988, 1989, and 1997.

22. Once again, it is important to remember that spending limits are almost always associated with public financing for candidates. As such, one must consider the effects of these two variables simultaneously.

23. The dummy year variables 1980, 1981, 1989, and 1997 were statistically significant in the Democratic spending equation, while 1985, 1986, 1988, 1989, 1993, 1996, and 1997 were significant in the Republican spending equation.

24. In an earlier analysis covering fewer years we found that it was the Democrats who were more adversely affected by spending limits. It may be the case that the partisan consequences may depend upon factors which are simply beyond the data currently available to us. So, for example, Malbin and Gais contend that Republicans are more likely to opt out of public financing and associated spending limits (see *The Day after Reform,* 62–65). If Republican candidates are increasingly less likely to participate in public financing and associated spending limits, then spending limits will continue to become more disassociated from actual spending. Unfortunately, we do not have data on the number of candidates who opted out of the public financing and spending limits options.

25. For a discussion of the financial advantage of incumbents in congressional elections and associated concerns with the differential effects of campaign finance reforms, see Goidel, Gross, and Shields, *Money Matters.* In our data set, incumbents running for governor had a mean spending per voting age citizen value of 1.34, while challengers had a mean value of .85.

26. The dummy year variables 1983, 1988, and 1997 were statistically significant at the .05 level for challenger spending, while 1980, 1983, 1991, 1995, and 1996 were statistically significant for incumbent spending.

27. None of the dummy year variables were statistically significant at the .10 level for the spending difference equation.

28. See Malbin and Gais, *The Day after Reform,* 66.

29. Of course, other things are usually not always equal. So, for example, in order to compensate for the so-called incumbency advantage, recent legislation in Vermont actually had lower spending limits for incumbents than for nonincumbents. From this perspective, equal funding would give incumbents a natural competitive advantage. Whether or not one

accepts this view, the important point is that, in many cases, the ultimate goal is electoral competition. Numerous campaign finance reform proposals are merely a means to this end.

## NOTES TO CHAPTER 5

1. See Herbert E. Alexander, *Financing Politics: Money, Elections, and Political Reform* (Washington, D.C.: Congressional Quarterly Press, 1992).

2. We should note that the figure includes both presidential and midterm election years, even though the number of incumbents running in presidential election years is quite small. We have excluded the handful of states that hold gubernatorial elections in odd-numbered years from this portion of the analysis.

3. For example, in 1978, the standard deviations for the margin of victory, the Democratic percentage of the vote, and the incumbent vote were 13.5, 10.5, and 8.4, respectively. Twenty years later in 1998, the standard deviations were 12.8, 11.4, and 8.4. See Gary Jacobson, "The Marginals Never Vanished: Incumbency and Competition in Elections to the U.S. House of Representatives, 1952–1982," *American Journal of Political Science* 31 (1987): 126–41.

4. See for example, Thad Beyle, ed., *Governors and Hard Times* (Washington, D.C: Congressional Quarterly Press, 1992).

5. Once again, the regression results portrayed in table 5.3 were generated using OLS with panel-corrected standard errors. The variables are defined as explained in chapter 4. The dummy year variables for 1992 and 1996 were statistically significant.

6. To get the effect on the margin of victory, we first take the expected effect on candidate spending based on the regression coefficients presented in table 4.4. For example, with limits set at a $1.00 per voting age citizen, Democratic spending would be expected to increase by $.44, while Republican spending would increase by approximately $.11. We then multiply these coefficients by the estimates presented in table 5.3. So, for example, assuming an open-seat election and a $1.00 per voting age citizen contribution limit, the effect of public financing on the margin of victory would be estimated by the following equation: $(1.7 \times 0.44) + (-4.7 \times 0.11) = +0.22$. The result would indicate that, under this particular scenario, the margin of victory would be expected to increase by about a fifth of one percent.

## NOTES TO CHAPTER 6

1. National trends are controlled for with the year dummy variables (see chapter 4), but are not included as part of table 6.2 so that the results are less cluttered by the year variables. The following years, however, are significant: 1985, 1991, 1996, and 1998.

2. The finding is similar to what has been observed in the congressional elections literature, and is likely to be subject to similar criticisms. That is, candidate spending is contemporaneously correlated with the error term of the regression model. Prior research has taken several different approaches to solving the simultanity problem, but none has been universally embraced. Within the gubernatorial elections literature, Partin employed a two-staged model and found that incumbent spending and challenger spending were roughly equivalent in effect. The first-stage regression models, however, were limited in terms of the explanatory power, leaving open questions as to the adequacy of the instrumental variables. Within this analysis, we have utilized OLS regression estimates, while accounting for the pooled time series nature of the data. At least within the congressional elections literature, OLS estimates have generally been the most conservative, at least when it comes to the implications for

reform. See Jacobson, *Money in Congressional Elections;* Green and Krasno, "Salvation for the Spendthrift Incumbent," 844–907; Goidel and Gross, "A Systems Approach to Campaign Finance in U.S. House Elections," 125–53; and Partin, "Assessing the Impact of Campaign Spending in Governor's Races."

3. Even if we assumed that incumbent and challenger spending are relatively equivalent in terms of their effects, we still would find only moderate effects on the incumbent share of the vote. Assuming that incumbent spending exerted an identical impact as challenger spending (b = 5.02) but in the opposite direction, we would expect the incumbent percentage of vote to decline with restrictive limits, but increase with less restrictive limits. For example, assuming a $.10 per voting age citizen limit, the incumbent vote would be expected to decrease by roughly 1.5 percent. Assuming a $1.00 per voting age citizen limit, incumbent spending would be expected to increase by 2.4 percent. With findings of equal spending effects, one would conclude that more restrictive limits better serve the objective of more competitive elections. Under findings of unequal effects (with incumbent spending relatively ineffective), one would conclude higher spending limits were more effective.

4. These estimates are obtained from the coefficients from chapter 4, using assumptions stated in the text. For example, the impact of providing public financing on incumbent spending is taken from the coefficient for public financing as presented in chapter 4 (–.54), indicating that on average incumbent spending is $.54 lower in states with public financing. We then combine this coefficient with the size of the limit (assuming, for example, a $1.00 per voting age citizen limit) multiplied by the coefficient for spending limits (1.1). The result is a total of +56, indicating that under this scenario incumbent spending increased by $.56. We then determine the impact of this change on the vote by multiplying the spending effect ($.56) by the coefficient for incumbent spending in the incumbent vote equation as presented in the current chapter. Finally, we do the same thing for challenger spending and then either add or subtract depending on the result. In this scenario, the result was a decline in the incumbent vote margin of just over a quarter of one percent.

5. See, for example, James L. Gibson, Cornelius P. Cotter, John F. Bibby, and Robert J. Huckshorn, "Assessing Party Organizational Strength," *American Journal of Political Science* 27 (1983): 193–222; Cornelius P. Cotter, James L. Gibson, John F. Bibby, and Robert Huckshorn, *Party Organization in the American Politics* (New York: Praeger, 1984); and Paul S. Herrnson, "Do Parties Make A Difference? The Role of Party Organizations in Congressional Elections," *Journal of Politics* 48 (1986): 589–615.

6. Ruth S. Jones, "State Public Campaign Finance: Implications for Partisan Politics," *American Journal of Political Science* 25 (1981): 342–61.

7. The following years were significant: 1982, 1988, 1989, and 1990.

8. In an earlier work, we found that studies of the effects of money in U.S. congressional elections which relied on OLS estimates were least supportive of reform, while studies that relied on instrumental variable techniques (2SLS, 3SLS) were more supportive. As such, the OLS estimates reported, more than likely, reflect conservative estimates, at least of the indirect effects in those elections involving incumbents. See Goidel and Gross, "Reconsidering the Myths and Realities," 129–50.

## NOTES TO CHAPTER 7

1. The research on registration requirements has been substantial. See, for example, Raymond E. Wolfinger and Stephen J. Rosenstone, *Who Votes?* (New Haven, Conn.: Yale University Press, 1980); Robert S. Erickson, "Why Do People Vote? Because They Are Regis-

tered," *American Politics Quarterly* 9 (1981): 259–76; G. Bingham Powell, "American Voter Turnout in Comparative Perspective," *American Political Science Review* 80 (1986): 17–44; Ruy A. Teixeira, *The Disappearing American Voter* (Washington, D.C.: Brookings Institute, 1992). Several studies have also provided more specific examinations of motor voter legislation. While there is some debate over the effect of motor voter legislation on registration and voting, most articles report a positive effect on registration and more limited effect on voting (and often an adverse effect on racial and income bias within the electorate). See, for example, Stephen Knack, "Does 'Motor Voter' Work? Evidence from State-Level Data," *Journal of Politics* 57 (1995): 796–811; Stephen Knack, "Drivers Wanted: Motor Voter and the Election of 1996," *PS, Political Science and Politics* 32 (1999): 237–43; Michael D. Martinez, "Did Motor Voter Work?" *American Politics Quarterly* 27 (1999): 296–315; and Raymond E. Wolfinger and Jonathan Hoffman, "Registering and Voting with Motor Voter," *PS, Political Science and Politics* 34 (2001): 85–92.

2. We should note that it is possible that midterm elections do both. With lower voter participation, there may also be fewer voters swayed by short-term (national) influences. See Angus Campbell, "Surge and Decline: A Study of Electoral Change," *Public Opinion Quarterly* 24 (1960):397–418; James E. Campbell, *The Presidential Pulse of Congressional Elections* (Lexington, Ky.: University of Kentucky Press, 1993).

3. For evidence supporting the link between negative advertising and turnout, see Stephen Ansolabehere, Shanto Iyengar, Adam Simon, and Nicholas Valentino, "Does Attack Advertising Demobilize the Electorate?" *American Political Science Review* 88 (1994): 829–38; and Stephen Ansolabehere, Shanto Iyengar, and Adam Simon, "Replicating Experiments Using Aggregate and Survey Data: The Case for Negative Advertising and Turnout," *American Political Science Review* 93 (1999): 901–909. For criticisms of this research, see Steven E. Finkel and John G. Geer, "A Spot Check: Casting Doubt on the Demobilizing Effect of Attack Advertising," *American Journal of Political Science* 42 (1998): 573–95; Martin P. Wattenberg and Craig Leonard Brians, "Negative Campaign Advertising: Demobilizer or Mobilizer?" *American Political Science Review* 93 (1999): 891–99; Paul Freedman and Ken Goldstein, "Measuring Media Exposure and the Effects of Negative Campaign Ads," *American Journal of Political Science* 43 (1999): 1189–1208; Richard R. Lau, Lee Sigelman, Caroline Heldman, and Paul Babbit, "The Effects of Negative Political Advertisements: A Meta-Analytic Assessment," *American Political Science Review* 93 (1999): 851–75. For a more qualified view, see Kim Fridkin Kahn and Patrick J. Kenney, "Do Negative Campaigns Mobilize or Suppress Turnout? Clarifying the Relationship between Negativity and Participation," *American Political Science Review* 93 (1999): 877–89.

4. See, for example, Charles H. Franklin, "Eschewing Obfuscation? Campaigns and the Perception of U.S. Senate Incumbents," *American Political Science Review* 85 (1991): 1193–1214; Goidel, Gross, and Shields, *Money Matters;* and Jon K. Dalager, "Voters, Issues, and Elections: Are the Candidates' Messages Getting Through?" *Journal of Politics* 58 (1996): 486–515. For a more positive assessment, though, see John J. Coleman and Paul F. Manna, "Congressional Campaign Spending and the Quality of Democracy," *Journal of Politics* 62 (2000): 757–89.

5. See Sara Fritz and Dwight Morris, *Gold-Plated Politics: Running for Congress in the 1990s* (Washington, D.C.: Congressional Quarterly Press, 1992); Dwight Morris and Murreille E. Gamache, *Gold-Plated Politics: The 1992 Congressional Races* (Washington, D.C.: Congressional Quarterly Press, 1994).

6. See Alan S. Gerber and Donald P. Green, "Do Phone Calls Increase Voter Turnout: A Field Experiment," *Public Opinion Quarterly* 65 (2001): 75–85; "The Effects of Canvassing, Telephone Calls, and Direct Mail on Voter Turnout: A Field Experiment," *American Political Science Review* 94 (2001): 653–63; and "The Effect of a Nonpartisan Get-Out-The-Vote Drive: An Experimental Study of Leafletting," *Journal of Politics* 62 (2000): 846–57.

7. Robert A. Jackson, "The Mobilization of U.S. State Electorates in the 1988 and 1990 Elections," *Journal of Politics* 59 (1997): 520–37; Robert Huckfeldt and John Sprague, "Political Parties and Electoral Mobilization: Political Structure, Social Structure, and the Party Canvas," *American Political Science Review* 86 (1992): 70–86; and Kim Quaile Hill and Jan E. Leighley, "Party Ideology, Organization, and Competitiveness as Mobilizing Forces in Gubernatorial Elections," *American Journal of Political Science* 37 (1993): 1158–98.

8. See Robert A. Jackson, "Voter Mobilization in the 1986 Midterm Election," *Journal of Politics* 55 (1993): 1081–99.

9. Voter turnout is computed as the percentage of voting age population. Because the population is always changing, it is difficult to get a precise estimate of the voting age population, particularly in the years between the censuses. We have estimated the voting age population using data from various issues of Michael Barone and Grant Ujifusa's *The Almanac of American Politics* (Washington, D.C.: National Journal) and Phil Duncan's *Politics in America* (Washington, D.C.: Congressional Quarterly Press).

10. See Patterson and Caldeira, "Getting Out the Vote," 675–89.

11. See Daniel J. Elazar, *American Federalism: A View from the States,* 3d ed. (New York: Harper & Row, 1984).

12. See Raymond E. Wolfinger and Stephen J. Rosenstone, *Who Votes?* (New Haven, Conn.: Yale University Press, 1980); and Teixeira, *The Disappearing American Voter.*

13. See Patterson and Caldeira, "Getting Out the Vote," 686.

14. See Gary W. Cox and Michael C. Munger, "Closeness, Expenditures, and Turnout in the 1982 U.S. House Elections," *American Political Science Review* 83 (1989): 217–31; Hill and Leighley, "Party Ideology, Organization, and Competitiveness," 1158–78; and Hill and Leighley, "Mobilizing Institutions and Class Representation in U.S. State Electorates," *Political Research Quarterly* 47 (1994): 137–50.

15. See Rosenstone and Hansen, *Mobilization, Participation, and Democracy in America.*

16. See Wolfinger and Rosenstone, *Who Votes?*

17. See Goidel, Gross, and Shields, *Money Matters.*

18. The following years were significant in the first model (which included all elections): 1980, 1984, 1985, 1988, 1992, and 1996. In the model that included only nonpresidential election years, the following years were significant: 1985, 1989, 1993, and 1997.

19. We also examined presidential election years separately. As with the Robert Jackson study of statewide voter turnout, we failed to find much evidence of political mobilization when we considered these elections alone.

20. In other analyses, we included the percentage of the state with a college education, the median age, and the percentage of the state that is rural. Because the measures were incomplete for the entire time series, we have not included these measures in the analysis presented in the text. Notably, with these measures included and for only 88 total cases, candidate campaign finance provisions are still associated with voter turnout at the .10 level (t = 1.85, p =.068).

21. Unlike Jackson's analysis of statewide voter turnout, we failed to find evidence of significant differences between incumbent and challenger spending. Presumably this discrepancy reflects differences in research design. Jackson utilized all fifty states in two election cycles, while we have included only states with gubernatorial elections, though we have done so over a broader time frame.

22. See John G. Peters and Susan Welch, "Politics, Corruption, and Political Culture: A View from the State Legislatures," *American Politics Quarterly* 6 (1978): 345–56; and David C. Nice, "Political Corruption in the American States," *American Politics Quarterly* 11 (1983): 507–17.

## NOTES TO CHAPTER 8

1. According to a March 2001 poll conducted by the Gallup Organization, 51 percent of Americans strongly favor "new federal laws limiting the amount of money that any individual or group can contribute to the national political parties." An additional 25 percent moderately favor such a proposal. Yet only 10 percent reported that they followed the debate over campaign finance reform "very closely." The results of Gallup opinion polls on campaign finance are available at www.gallup.com/poll/indicators/indcamp_fin.asp.

2. According to an October 2000 Gallup poll, 34 percent of Americans place greater priority on "protecting the freedom of individuals to support political candidates and parties" than on "protecting government from excessive influence by campaign contributors."

3. See Goidel, Gross, and Shields, *Money Matters,* 35.

4. The exact nature of the bias is unclear. Similar findings at the congressional level have been used to justify the positions of both supporters and opponents of public financing and spending limits. One attempt to overcome the incumbency advantage is the law in Vermont which effectively places lower spending limits on incumbents than on challengers.

5. See Malbin and Gais, *The Day after Reform.*

6. The fact that spending did not seem to be affected by the level of a state's contribution limits (see chapter 4) may be due to the fact that high-end contributors, those who give $500 or more, are a limited pool.

7. Another effect of contribution limits may be to further reduce the candidate pool to self-financed candidates who are able to exit the campaign finance system and spend their own money. However, to date the so-called debilitating effects of restrictive contribution limits have not been realized in the states, nor for that matter have the positive effects of unlimited contribution limits. Put simply, states with unlimited contribution limits are no more competitive than states with such restrictions.

8. While the results in this text are not as definitive as those in our book on congressional elections, in many ways, the conclusion is similar. See Goidel, Gross, and Shields, *Money Matters.*

9. One of the more innovative aspects of the Vermont law is that spending limits are effectively lower for incumbents than for nonincumbents.

10. Marc Cooper, "Clean Money in Maine," *Nation* 21 (2000): 22–24; "The Impact of Clean Elections on Arizona's 2000 Election," a report by the Arizona Clean Elections Institute, 23 April 23 2001; and Joshua Green, "Clean Money in Maine," *American Prospect* 21 (2000): 36–38.

11. Quoted in Green, "Clean Money in Maine."

12. We do have estimates, but those are limited to individual states over a limited period of time. For example, in the 2000 legislative elections in Maine, about a third of all general election candidates opted for clean money. In races where they faced opponents who decided to forego the clean money option, over half of these candidates won election. As Malbin and Gais have reported, more Republicans than Democrats opted out of the Clean Money campaign finance system. See, for example, Green, "Clean Money"; Cooper, "Clean Money"; and Malbin and Gais, *The Day after Reform.*

13. See Green, "Clean Money"; and Cooper, "Clean Money."

# References

Abramowitz, Alan. 1991. "Incumbency, Campaign Spending, and the Decline of Competition in U.S. House Elections." *Journal of Politics* 53:34–56.

Alexander, Herbert, and Laura Denny. 1966. *Regulation of Political Finance.* Princeton, N.J.: Citizens Research Foundation.

Allen, Mike. 2000. "Campaign Secrecy Law's Impact Doubted." *Washington Post.* 1 July, A6.

Ansolabehere, Stephen, Shanto Iyengar, and Adam Simon. 1999. "Replicating Experiments Using Aggregate and Survey Data: The Case for Negative Advertising and Turnout." *American Political Science Review* 93: 901–909.

Ansolabehere, Stephen, Shanto Iyengar, Adam Simon, and Nicholas Valentino. 1994. "Does Attack Advertising Demobilize the Electorate?" *American Political Science Review* 88: 829–38.

Barone, Michael, and Grant Ujifusa. [Various years]. *The Almanac of American Politics.* Washington, D.C.: National Journal.

Beck, Nathaniel, and Jonathan N. Katz. 1995. "What to Do (and Not to Do) with Time-Series Cross-Section Data." *American Political Science Review* 89: 634–47.

Beiler, David. 1999. "The Body Politic Registers a Protest." *Campaigns and Elections* 20: 34–43.

Beyle, Thad. 1983. "The Cost of Becoming Governor." *State Government* 56: 74–84.

———. 1986. "The Cost of Becoming Governor." *State Government* 59: 95–101.

———. 1992. "The Cost of Becoming Governor." *State Government* 65: 15–20.

———. 1992. *Governors and Hard Times.* Washington, D.C.: Congressional Quarterly Press.

Blalock, Hubert M. 1979. *Social Statistics.* New York: McGraw-Hill.

Box-Steffensmeier, Janet. 1996. "A Dynamic Analysis of the Role of War Chests in Campaign Strategy." *American Journal of Political Science* 40: 352–71.

Brooks, Jackson. 1990. *Broken Promises: Why the Federal Election Commission Failed.* New York: Priority Press.

*Buckley v. Valeo.* 1976. 424 U.S. 1.

Campbell, Angus. 1960. "Surge and Decline: A Study of Electoral Change." *Public Opinion Quarterly* 24: 397–418.

Campbell, James E. 1993. *The Presidential Pulse of Congressional Elections.* Lexington, Ky.: University of Kentucky Press.

Carpini, Michael X. Delli, and Scott Keeter. 1996. *What Americans Know and Why It Matters.* New Haven, Conn.: Yale University Press.

Chappell, Henry. 1982. "Campaign Contributions and Congressional Voting: A Simultaneous Probit-Tobit Model." *Review of Economics and Statistics* 62: 77–83.

Coleman, John J., and Paul F. Manna. 2000. "Congressional Campaign Spending and the Quality of Democracy." *Journal of Politics* 62: 757–89.

Cooper, Marc. 2000. "Clean Money in Maine." *Nation* 21: 22–24.

Cotter, Cornelius P., James L. Gibson, John F. Bibby, and Robert J. Huckshorn. 1984. *Party Organization in American Politics.* New York: Praeger.

Cox, Gary W., and Michael C. Munger. 1989. "Closeness, Expenditures and Turnout in the 1982 U.S. House Elections." *American Political Science Review* 83: 217–31.

Crowley, Michael, and Frank Phillips. 2000. "Mass. House Waters Down Key Reforms." *Boston Globe,* 15 April, A1.

Dalager, Jon K. 1996. "Voters, Issues, and Elections: Are Candidates' Messages Getting Through?" *Journal of Politics* 58: 486–515.

Donnay, Patrick, and Graham Ramsden. 1995. "Public Financing of Legislative Elections: Lessons from Minnesota." *Legislative Studies Quarterly* 20: 351–64.

Drew, Elizabeth. 1999. *The Corruption of American Politics: What Went Wrong and Why.* Secaucus, N.J.: Carol Publishing Group.

Dreyfuss, Robert. 1998. "Reform beyond the Beltway: States as Laboratories of Clean Money." *American Prospect* 31: 50–55.

Duncan, Phil. n.d. *Politics in America.* Washington, D.C.: Congressional Quarterly Press.

Elazar, Daniel J. 1984. *American Federalism: A View from the States.* 3d ed. New York: Harper & Row.

Erikson, Robert S. 1981. "Why Do People Vote? Because They Are Registered." *American Politics Quarterly* 9: 259–76.

Evans, Diana. 1986. "PAC Contributions and Roll Call Voting: Conditional Power." In *Interest Group Politics.* 2d ed. Edited by Allan Cigler and Burdette Loomis. Washington, D.C.: Congressional Quarterly Press.

Finkel, Steven E., and John G. Geer. 1998. "A Spot Check: Casting Doubt on the Demobilizing Effect of Attack Advertising." *American Journal of Political Science* 42: 573–95.

Franklin, Charles H. 1991. "Eschewing Obfuscation? Campaigns and the Perception of U.S. Senate Incumbents." *American Political Science Review* 85: 1193–1214.

Freeman, Paul, and Ken Goldstein. 1999. "Measuring Media Exposure and the Effects of Negative Campaign Ads." *American Journal of Political Science* 43: 1189–1208.

Fritz, Sara, and Dwight Morris. 1992. *Gold-Plated Politics: Running for Congress in the 1990s.* Washington, D.C.: Congressional Quarterly Press.

Gaddie, Keith. 1997. "Forgotten Races: Open Seat Congressional Elections." Unpublished manuscript.

Gerber, Alan S., and Donald P. Green. 2001. "Do Phone Calls Increase Voter Turnout: A Field Experiment." *Public Opinion Quarterly* 65: 75–85.

———. 2001. "The Effects of Canvassing, Telephone Calls, and Direct Mail on Voter Turnout: A Field Experiment." *American Political Science Review* 94: 653–63.

———. 2000. "The Effects of a Nonpartisan Get-Out-The-Vote Drive: An Experimental Study of Leafletting." *Journal of Politics* 62: 846–57.

Gibson, James L., Cornelius P. Cotter, John F. Bibby, and Robert J. Huckshorn. 1983. "Assessing Party Organizational Strength." *American Journal of Political Science* 27: 193–222.

Gierzynski, Anthony. 1998. "Data Gathering Issues." In *Campaign Finance in State Legislative Elections.* Edited by Joel Thompson and Gary Moncrief. Washington, D.C.: Congressional Quarterly Press.

———. 2000. *Money Rules: Financing Elections in America.* Boulder, Colo.: Westview Press.

Goidel, Robert K., and Donald A. Gross. 1994. "A Systems Approach to Campaign Finance in U.S. House Elections." *American Politics Quarterly* 22: 125–53.

————. 1996. "Reconsidering the Myths and Realities of Campaign Finance Reform." *Legislative Studies Quarterly* 21: 129–50.

Goidel, Robert K., Donald A. Gross, and Todd G. Shields. 1999. *Money Matters: Consequences of Campaign Finance Reform in U.S. House Elections.* Boulder, Colo.: Rowman & Littlefield.

Goldberg, Deborah. 1998. *Writing Reform: A Guide to Drafting State and Local Campaign Finance Laws.* New York: Brennan Center for Justice.

Green, Donald, and Jonathan Krasno. 1998. "Salvation for the Spendthrift Incumbent." *American Journal of Political Science* 32: 844–907.

Green, John, Paul Herrnson, Lynda Powell, and Clyde Wilcox. 2001. "Individual Congressional Campaign Contributors: Wealthy, Conservative and Reform-Minded." Unpublished manuscript, available on the internet at www.bsos.umd.edu

————. 1999. "Women Big donors Mobilized in Congressional Reform." Unpublished paper, available on the internet at www.bsos.umd.edu

Green, Joshua. 2000. "Clean Money in Maine." *American Prospect* 21: 36–38.

Grenzke, Janet. 1990. "Shopping in the Congressional Supermarket: The Currency Is Complex." *American Journal of Political Science* 33: 1–24.

Gross, Donald A. 1981. "Problems in Making Meaningful Comparisons: A Research Note." *Humbolt Journal of Social Relations* 8.

Hall, Richard, and Frank Wayman. "Buying Time: Moneyed Interests and the Mobilization of Bias in Congressional Committees." *American Political Science Review* 84: 797–820.

Herrnson, Paul S. 1986. "Do Parties Make A Difference? The Role of Party Organizations in Congressional Elections." *Journal of Politics* 48: 589–615.

————. 1998. *Congressional Elections: Campaigning at Home and in Washington.* Washington, D.C.: Congressional Quarterly Press.

Hill, Kim Quaile, and Jan E. Leighley. 1993. "Party Ideology, Organization, and Competitiveness as Mobilizing Forces in Gubernatorial Elections." *American Journal of Political Science* 37: 1158–98.

————. 1994. "Mobilizing Institutions and Class Representation in U.S. State Electorates." *Political Research Quarterly* 47: 137–50.

Hogan, Robert. 1999. "Campaign Spending in State Legislative Primary Elections." *State and Local Government Review* 31: 214–40.

————. [2001?] "The Costs of Representation in State Legislatures: Explaining Variations in Campaign Spending." *Social Science Quarterly.*

Holbrook, Thomas, and Emily Van Dunk. 1993. "Electoral Competition in the American States." *American Political Science Review* 87: 955–62.

Huckfeldt, Robert, and John Sprague. 1992. "Political Parties and Electoral Mobilization: Political Structure, Social Structure, and the Party Canvas." *American Political Science Review* 86: 70–86.

Jackson, Robert A. 1993. "Voter Mobilization in the 1986 Midterm Election." *Journal of Politics* 55: 1081–99.

————. 1997. "The Mobilization of U.S. State Electorates in the 1988 and 1990 Elections." *Journal of Politics* 59: 520–37.

Jacobson, Gary. 1980. *Money in Congressional Elections.* New Haven, Conn.: Yale University Press.

————. 1987. "The Marginals Never Vanished: Incumbency and Competition in Elections to the U.S. House of Representatives." *American Journal of Political Science* 31: 126–41.

Jacobson, Gary, and Samuel Kernell. 1983. *Strategy and Choice in Congressional Elections.* 2d ed. New Haven, Conn.: Yale University Press.

Jewell, Malcolm, and David Olson. 1988. *Political Parties and Elections in American States.* 3d ed. Chicago: Dorsey Press.

Jewell, Malcolm, and William Cassie. 1998. "Can the Legislative Campaign Finance System Be Reformed?" In *Campaign Finance in State Legislative Elections.* Edited by Joel Tompson and Gary Moncrief. Washington, D.C.: Congressional Quarterly Press.

Jones, Ruth. 1984. "Financing State Elections." In *Money and Politics in the United States: Financing Elections in the 1980s.* Edited by Michael Malbin. Chatham, N.J.: Chatham House.

———. 1994. "U.S. State-Level Campaign Finance Reform." In *Comparative Political Finance among the Democracies.* Edited by Herbert Alexander and Rei Shiratori. Boulder, Colo.: Westview Press.

Jones, Woodrow, and K. Robert Keiser. 1987. "Issue Visibility and the Effects of PAC Money." *Social Science Quarterly* 68: 170–76.

Kahn, Kim. 1995. "Characteristics of Press Coverage in Senate and Gubernatorial Elections: Information Available to Voters." *Legislative Studies Quarterly* 20: 1–23.

Kahn, Kim, and Patrick J. Kenney. 1999. "Do Negative Campaigns Mobilize or Suppress Turnout?" *American Political Science Review* 93: 877–89.

Knack, Stephen. 1999. "Does Motor Voter Work? Evidence from State-Level Data." *Journal of Politics* 57: 796–811.

———. 1999. "Drivers Wanted: Motor Voter and the Election of 1996." *PS, Political Science and Politics* 32: 237–43.

Krasno, Jonathan, and Donald P. Green. 1993. "Stopping the Buck Here: The Case for Campaign Spending Limits." *Brookings Review:* 17–21.

Landbein, Laura, and Mark Lotwis. 1990. "The Political Efficacy of Lobbying and Money: Gun Control in the U.S. House." *Legislative Studies Quarterly* 14: 414–40.

Lau, Richard R., Lee Sigelman, Caroline Heldman, and Paul Babbit. 1999. "The Effects of Negative Political Advertisements: A Meta-Analytic Assessment." *American Political Science Review* 93: 851–75.

Lowenstein, Hays. 1989. "On Campaign Finance Reform: The Root of All Evil Is Deeply Rooted." *Hofstra Law Review* 301.

Magelby, David. 2001. *Election Advocacy: Soft Money and Issue Advocacy in the 2000 Congressional Elections.* Report funded by the Pew Charitable Trusts. Salt Lake City: Brigham Young University.

Malbin, Michael. 1995. "Most GOP Winners Spent Enough Money to Reach Voters." *Political Finance and Lobby Reporter* (January): 11.

Malbin, Michael, and Thomas Gais. 1998. *The Day after Reform: Sobering Campaign Finance Lesson from the American States.* Albany, N.Y.: Rockefeller Institute Press.

Martinez, Michael D. 1999. "Did Motor Voter Work?" *American Politics Quarterly* 27: 296–315.

Mayer, Kenneth. 1997. *Campaign Finance Reform in the States: A Report to the Governor's Blue Ribbon Commission on Campaign Finance Reform.* Report funded by the Pew Charitable Trusts. Salt Lake City: Brigham Young University.

Mayer, Kenneth, and John Wood. 1995. "The Impact of Public Financing on Electoral Competitiveness: Evidence from Wisconsin, 1964–1990." *Legislative Studies Quarterly* 20: 69–88.

McIver, John, and Edward Carmines. 1981. *Unidimensional Scaling.* Beverly Hills, Calif.: Sage Publications.

Miller, Ellen, and Joshua Rosenkranz. 1998. "How Was Campaign-Finance Reform Killed? By Twisting What the High Court Said; Free Speech and Campaign Myth." *Nation* 266: 22–25.

Neuborne, Burt. 1998. *Campaign Finance Reform and the Constitution: A Critical Look at Buckley v. Valeo.* New York: Brennan Center for Justice.

Overacker, Louise. 1932. *Money in Elections.* New York: Macmillan.

Partin, Randall. 1999. "Assessing the Impact of Campaign Spending in Governor's Races." Paper presented at the annual meeting of the American Political Science Association, Atlanta, Ga.

Patterson, Samuel. 1982. "Campaign Spending in Contest for Governor." *Western Political Quarterly* 35: 457–77.

Patterson, Samuel, and Gregory Caldeira. 1983. "Getting Out the Vote: Participation in Gubernatorial Elections. *American Political Science Review* 77: 675–99.

Peters, John G., and Susan Welch. 1978. "Politics, Corruption, and Political Culture: A View from the State Legislatures." *American Politics Quarterly* 11:507–17.

Pomper, Gerald M. 2001. *The Election of 2000.* New York: Chatham House Publishers.

Powell, G. Bingham. 1986. "American Voter Turnout in Comparative Perspective." *American Political Science Review* 80: 17–44.

Ranney, Austin. 1976. "Parties in State Politics." In *Politics in the American States,* edited by Herbert Jacob and Kenneth Vines. 3d ed. Boston: Little, Brown & Co.

Redfield, Kent. 1996. "The Good, the Bad, and the Perfect: Searching for Campaign Finance Reform in Illinois." *Spectrum: Journal of State Government* 69: 38–42.

Rosenkranz, Joshua. 1998. *Buckley Stops Here: Loosening the Judicial Stranglehold on Campaign Finance Reform.* Washington, D.C.: Twentieth Century Fund.

Rosenstone, Steven, and John Hansen. 1993. *Mobilization, Participation, and Democracy in America.* New York: Macmillan.

Rothenberg, Lawrence. 1992. *Linking Citizens to Government: Interest Group Politics at Common Cause.* New York: Cambridge University Press.

Sabato, Larry, and Glenn Simpson. 1996. *Dirty Little Secrets.* New York: Random House.

Sayrs, Louis. 1989. *Pooled Time Series Analysis.* Newbury Park, Calif.: Sage Publications.

Schier, Steven. 1999. "Jesse's Victory." *Washington Monthly* 31: 8–13.

Schroedeul, Jean. 1987. "Campaign Contributions and Legislative Outcomes." *Western Political Quarterly* 40: 371–89.

Shields, Todd, and Robert Goidel. "Who Contributes? Checkbook Participation, Class Biases, and the Impact of Legal Reforms, 1952–1994." *American Politics Quarterly* 28: 216–33.

Smith, Bradley. 1995. "Faulty Assumptions and Undemocratic Consequences of Campaign Finance Reform." *Yale Law Review* 105: 1049–91.

Sorauf, Frank. 1988. *Money in American Elections.* Glenview, IL: Scott, Foresman.

———. 1992. *Inside Campaign Finance Reform: Myths and Realities.* New Haven, Conn.: Yale University Press.

Squire, Peverill. 1991. "Preemptive Fundraising and Challenger Profile in Senate Elections." *Journal of Politics* 53: 1150–64.

———. 1992. "Challenger Profile and Gubernatorial Elections." *Western Political Quarterly* 45: 124–42.

Squire, Peverill, and Christina Fastnow. 1994. "Comparing Gubernatorial and Senatorial Elections." *Political Research Quarterly* 47: 703–20.

Stimson, James. 1985. "Regression in Space and Time: A Statistical Essay." *American Journal of Political Science* 29: 914–47.

REFERENCES

Stratmann, Thomas. 1991. "What Do Campaign Contributions Buy? Deciphering Causal Effects of Money and Votes." *Southern Economic Journal* (January).

———. 1995. "Campaign Contributions and Congressional Voting: Does the Timing of Contributions Matter?" *Review of Economics and Statistics* (January).

———. 1996. "How Reelection Constituencies Matter: Evidence from Political Action Committees' Contributions and Congressional Voting." *Journal of Law and Economics* (October).

Svoboda, Craig. 1995. "How and Why Voters Vote in Gubernatorial Elections." Doctoral dissertation University of Wisconsin-Milwaukee.

Teixeira, Ruy A. 1992. *The Disappearing American Voter.* Washington, D.C.: Brookings Institute.

Thayer, George. 1973. *Who Shakes the Money Tree.* New York: Simon & Schuster.

Thompson, Joel, and Gary Moncrief. 1998. *Campaign Finance in State Legislative Elections.* Washington, D.C.: Congressional Quarterly Press.

Verba, Sydney, Kay Schlozman, and Henry Brady. *Voice and Equality: Civic Voluntarism in American Politics.* Boston: Harvard University Press.

Wattenberg, Martin P., and Craig Leonard Brians. 1999. "Negative Campaign Advertising: Demobilizer or Mobilizer?" *American Political Science Review* 93: 891–99.

Welch, William. 1982. "Campaign Contributions and Legislative Voting: Milk Money and Dairy Supports." *Western Political Quarterly* 35: 478–95.

West, Darrell, and Burdett Loomis. 1998. *The Sound of Money: How Political Interests Get What They Want.* New York: W.W. Norton.

Wolfinger, Raymond E., and Jonathan Hoffman. 2001. "Registering and Voting with Motor Voter." *PS, Political Science and Politics* 34: 85–92.

Wolfinger, Raymond E., and Stephen J. Rosenstone. 1980. *Who Votes?* New Haven, Conn.: Yale University Press.

Wright, John. 1985. "PACs, Contributions, and Roll Calls: An Organizational Perspective." *American Political Science Review* 79: 400–414.

———. 1990. "Contributions, Lobbying, and Committee Voting in the U.S. House of Representatives." *American Political Science Review* 84: 417–38.

———. 1996. *Interest Groups and Congress: Lobbying, Contributions, and Influence.* Boston: Allyn & Bacon.

# Index